AMERICAN PHILOSOPHY

AMERICAN PHILOSOPHY

from Edwards to Quine

edited and with an Introduction by
Robert W. Shahan and
Kenneth R. Merrill

UNIVERSITY OF OKLAHOMA PRESS : *Norman*

Library of Congress Cataloging in Publication Data
Main entry under title:

American philosophy from Edwards to Quine.

Includes bibliographical references and index.
1. Philosophy, American—Addresses, essays, lectures.
I. Shahan, Robert W., 1935–   II. Merrill,
Kenneth R.
B851.A47   191   76–62515
ISBN 0–8061–1395–2

Preface

It is almost impertinent to praise the philosophers whose views are discussed in this book, and yet the temptation to do so is strong. We have decided to compromise by adding a brief word of explanation—surely no justification is needed—for our choice of Jonathan Edwards, Ralph Waldo Emerson and Henry David Thoreau, the Pragmatists, Josiah Royce, George Santayana, and Willard Van Orman Quine.

Edwards is without rival as the greatest philosopher/theologian of colonial America. Before Emerson, no other thinker remotely approaches Edwards in intellectual endowment, range of interests, or depth and subtlety of treatment of a variety of philosophical topics. Emerson and Thoreau together represent the high point of American transcendentalism, a philosophy that is at once quixotic and endlessly fascinating. The triumvirate of Charles Sanders Peirce, William James, and John Dewey—the Big Three of American pragmatism—form a constellation of philosophers whose like has been seen neither before nor since their time. The brilliant, irascible Peirce may well be the greatest philosopher America has produced. Philosophical idealism reached its American zenith in Josiah Royce, a thinker whose vast erudition and formidable intelligence breathed new life—temporarily, as it turned out—into a point of view widely thought to be moribund. George Santayana is, with Emerson, the poet of American philosophy. Anyone with an ear for the music of well-written English can be captivated by Santayana's style, even while disagreeing with just about everything he says. But, as the essay in this book clearly shows, Santayana is more than a poet; he has important philosophical things to say.

It is a pleasure to be able to say that W. V. Quine, unlike the other philosophers discussed, is very much alive. Quine is one of America's most distinguished living philosophers and very probably the most influential.

The men whose essays appear in this volume were chosen because they have demonstrated unusual competence in at least one of the philosophies treated. All the essays are new, and each represents a substantial contribution to the literature on American philosophy.

The essays in this book were read by their authors at the sixth annual Oklahoma Conference on Philosophy held at the University of Oklahoma, March 31 to April 3, 1976. The editors wish to express their gratitude to the Conference participants—Roland Delattre, Robert Caponigri, Max Fisch, Peter Fuss, Frederick Olafson and W. V. Quine—for their excellent papers and lively discussions, and for the genuine pleasure of their company.

Robert W. Shahan

Kenneth R. Merrill

Contents

vii

FROM EDWARDS TO QUINE

Introduction

There is, of course, no substitute for reading the following essays themselves. No summary can do justice to the detailed expositions and arguments to be found in them. However, nonomnivorous readers—as well as those whose time is limited—may be grateful for a few editorial guideposts. The following summaries, which are somewhat longer than those usually found in an introduction, are offered in the hope they may be useful to such readers.

"Beauty and Politics: A Problematic Legacy of Jonathan Edwards" is the apt title of Roland A. Delattre's exploration of two facets of the thought of America's first philosophical-theological genius. The title is apt in that both themes (beauty and politics) are problematic for the student of Edwards, but they are problematic for different reasons. The problem with regard to beauty is that, in spite of Edwards' undisguised preoccupation with that concept, its central importance in Edwards' thought is insufficiently appreciated. The problem with regard to politics is that Edwards shows little interest in it or in political institutions.

Accordingly, Delattre has two main tasks: (1) to demonstrate the "absolutely fundamental" place of beauty in Edwards' vision of reality, and (2) to work out, on Edwards' behalf, the implications of that vision for politics. Although the first task is interesting and important in its own right, Delattre undertakes it primarily as a necessary condition of locating the aesthetic foundations of the (largely implicit) Edwardsean political legacy.

Though Edwards himself has scant interest in political matters as such, the Great Awakening (of which Edwards is the chief figure) is regarded by some historians as the religious precursor of the American Revolution thirty-five or forty years later. The challenge to ecclesiastical and colonial political power embodied in that religious revival prefigured, and helped to prepare the ground for, the break with England in the 1770's.

One can only make an educated guess as to how Edwards, who died in 1758, would have reacted to the War of Independence. What is clear is that even Edwards' most devout followers seldom appreciated the radical character of his aesthetic theology, specifically his conviction that God exercises his sovereign power primarily through "the attractive and creative and re-creative power of his own beauty" rather than through the terror of threatened punishment or quasi-mechanical force. For Edwards, the first principle of being is beauty, the highest form of which is the "cordial or affectional consent to being in general." Secondary or natural beauty, whose essence consists in harmony and proportion, is an image of primary or spiritual beauty.

To bring the notion of beauty closer to the principle of political order, Delattre offers an analysis of Edwards' dictum that "the will always is as the greatest apparent good is." One of the virtues of Delattre's analysis is that it scuttles the widespread misconception that Edwards holds to a crudely deterministic theory of will. The will is not determined by anything other than its own pleasure; it is "in correspondence with its object, the apparent good," where "apparent good" is a synonym for "beauty."

Edwards uses the notion of consent to being in his theory of community, which represents a grander beauty than that in virtuous individuals considered in themselves. Unfortunately, Edwards tends to "resolve or sublimate political into social or familial or religious terms"; he does little to extend these manifestations of "being's cordial consent to being" to an expressly political conception.

The rest of Delattre's essay is devoted to sketching an Edwardsean politics—a politics in which political order, like the personal order of virtue, is a kind of beauty. Those who see Edwards as an authoritarian defender of God's sovereignty will be surprised to learn that personal freedom and the rejection of arbitrary authority are integral parts of the Edwardsean political scheme. (But then Edwards' concept of God's sovereignty is itself often misunderstood, as Delattre convincingly showed earlier.) However, Edwards' political economy, as Delattre fills it in for us, allows for the orderly resolution of tensions and conflicts, which are unavoidable in a political community. Indeed, diversity is *required* for beauty—and for politics. The plurality of human beings is real, and is set in a network of relations that extend throughout the whole system of being. It is important, therefore, that the arena of politics be preserved in its integrity. Though Edwards sees history teleologically, an Edwardsean political philosophy will stress the responsible experience of present realities in their manifold degrees of beauty and deformity quite as much as the vision of some future kingdom of God on earth.

"Individual, Civil Society, and State in American Transcendentalism" is Robert Caponigri's exploration of several intertwined themes in the philosophies of Emerson, Thoreau, and, to a lesser extent, Orestes Brownson. More specifically, Caponigri examines the implications of what he calls the transcendentalist principle for civil society; he also examines the efforts of these three men to mitigate some of the most unpalatable of such consequences.

The transcendentalist principle is an extreme form of epistemological individualism, which makes a curious companion for the pantheism of which the transcendentalists were often suspected. The individual is the final repository of truth, which is communicated directly by intuition. The truths thus received are not private in any idiosyncratic sense; they are universally valid. Emerson expressed this vision of truth simply and plainly: "To believe your own thought, to believe that what is true in your private heart is true for all men—that is genius." But if these truths are not disablingly subjective, neither are they under the control of the recipient; they are communicated unpredictably, episodically.

Our initial fear that this radical individualism will undermine the foundations of the civil order is temporarily allayed when we are assured that the truths welling up in one private heart also well up in every other private heart. On further reflection, however, we find that our earlier misgivings were justified after all. The inevitable result of transcendentalism is the dissolution of the idea of civil order.

Thoreau observes, rightly, that morality and policy—or, as we may also put it, conscience and coercive power—are not the same. What neither Thoreau nor Emerson can provide—though they try—is a principle by which the conflicting claims of individual conscience and public necessity can be both preserved and mediated. The elements by which a civil order is constituted and sustained—the public philosophy, history, tradition, and authority—have no place in the transcendentalist scheme. The coincidence of the various private truths is, in Caponigri's apt term, "occasionalistic." There is no law or principle by which the coincidence is regulated and assured, and no principled basis for neutralizing the potentially calamitous results of noncoincidence. History, tradition, and authority suffer a similar fate: they are banished from transcendentalism as the repressive foes of individual freedom and truth.

The consequences of the dissolution of the principle of the state are principally two: (1) the state as the agent of policy and of civil order is reduced to expediency, and (2) morality and policy, conscience and power, remain in that condition of unmediated confrontation and alienation which the civil order was designed to heal. For the transcendentalist, the state is an institutional expression of the darker, unillumined side of human nature; its authority has no moral basis. There is, to be sure, a kind of bitter necessity to the state—a necessity rooted in the intermittency and evanescence of that inner revelation of universal mind. But genuine morality, conscience, truth— these are the nontransferable birthright of the individual, given through a kind of grace that can be neither forced nor foreseen. Here indeed is a Manichean vision of the human soul as sundered into realms of light and darkness, irreconcilably at war.

But Emerson and Thoreau try to heal the breach— Emerson through his concept of the elitism of character and the myth of the wise man, Thoreau by the notion of resistance to civil government. Through an unfortunate editorial error, the title of Thoreau's famous address "Resistance to Civil Government" was changed to "Civil Disobedience," a phrase that obscures the positive character of resistance. Resistance, in Thoreau's view, is intended not merely to draw limits to the expediency of the state, but "to release the power of truth into the realm of policy," much in the manner of Gandhi's notion of "Satyagraha," "the force of truth." But for all their efforts to mollify the harshness of the conflict between individual and state, Emerson and Thoreau are afflicted with a kind of intellectual astigmatism (or, to modify Caponigri's ocular metaphor slightly, a kind of intellectual scotoma) that is an inescapable consequence of the transcendentalist principle. It remained for Orestes Brownson to reformulate the principle so as to admit the elements of public truth, history, tradition, and authority upon which civil society rests.

Taking the distinction between the written and unwritten constitution as a pivot, Brownson criticizes the founding fathers of this nation for not recognizing what they had done. They failed to see that a written constitution, however good, can be legitimized only by an authority that is not derived from that very constitution—in this case, the authority of the American people or civil society. This people or civil society cannot be identified with either the government or the abstract individual. Rather, the civil society, whose formation is a long and complex historical process, establishes the just powers and limits of the state and the freedom of the individual. The claims of governmental authority and personal autonomy are balanced in a dialectical union of morality and policy—a union which Emerson and Thoreau, by reason of their blinkering transcendentalist principle, could not achieve.

The year 1898 is the watershed of American pragmatism, because, among other reasons, it was the year in which William James christened the movement. Such is the thesis of Max H. Fisch in his essay "American Pragmatism before and after 1898." Unlike Juliet, who believed a rose by any other name would smell as sweet, Fisch holds that the *name* "pragmatism" was important; it "served both as a flag for its followers and as a target for its critics." Taking James's address to the Philosophical Union of the University of California ("Philosophical Conceptions and Practical Results") as his starting point, Fisch first tries to trace pragmatism back to its origins thirty or more years earlier; he then moves forward through its post-1898 period.

With typical generosity, James credits Charles Sanders Peirce with not only providing the philosophical ideas underlying pragmatism but also supplying the name. James's own choice for a name is "practicalism"—a choice that reflects his sense of the differences between his views and those of Peirce. For one thing, Peirce looked on pragmatism as the natural outcome of reflecting on the methods of science, whereas James always construed the "principle of pragmatism" more broadly. In "How to Make Our Ideas Clear" (1878) Peirce shows how "the pragmatic maxim" (as he later called it) can be applied to such familiar notions as hardness, weight, and force, as well as to such philosophically central notions as reality and truth. In other papers Peirce seeks to make more difficult applications of the rule, for example, to probability. James is equally ready to try it on religious and moral issues.

In looking for the beginnings of pragmatism, Fisch takes the reader through a series of papers in which both the development and the recurring themes of Peirce's thought become progressively clearer. For one thing, it occurs to us that Peirce is seeking to supplant Descartes' *Discourse on Method* with his own distinctively anti-Cartesian method. He never finished his post-Darwinian version of the *Discourse*, in part because he was forced to rethink the whole enterprise during his years at The Johns Hopkins University—"in the company of the brightest, the most advanced, and the most serious students of logic anywhere in the country, perhaps in the world." Nonetheless, the evidence (contained in Peirce's writings in the late 1860's and early 1870's) suggests unmistakably that Peirce had committed to print the essential structure of pragmatism by 1868. Thus, it is quite plausible that James may have heard Peirce expounding something very like a full-blown pragmatism in the early 1870's, as James appears to imply in his 1898 address; and it is even likely that Peirce may have used the *term* "pragmatism" at that time.

Fisch examines more briefly the earlier expressions of pragmatism in James and Oliver Wendell Holmes, Jr. In the case of James, it is fairly easy to sort out what he owes to Peirce's writings and what he owes to Peirce's "philosophical companionship in old times" (as he phrases it in his Philosophical Union paper). But while Holmes is plainly a legal pragmatist as early as 1872, it is not clear just what, if anything, he owes to Peirce and what, if anything, Peirce owes to him.

In the years following 1898, pragmatism was very much in the air, not only in America but in England and Italy as well. Among those who were making a mark on the philosophical world are John Dewey, F. C. S. Schiller (an Englishman, not a German, in spite of the name), and Josiah Royce, who called himself an absolute pragmatist. The fullest expression of Royce's debt to pragmatism, especially the Peircean brand, is *The Problem of Christianity*, in which Royce makes extensive use of Peirce's general theory of signs in working out his own theory of the Community of Interpretation. One of Royce's most distinguished students, C. I. Lewis, developed a variant of pragmatism which he (Lewis) qualified with the adjective "conceptualistic." Among those still living, W. V. Quine has been called "the last pragmatist." But if Fisch is right, the "last" pragmatist has by no means yet appeared. Other philosophers coming on will be glad to bear the name.

Peter Fuss (in "Royce on the Concept of the Self: A His-

torical and Critical Perspective") seeks to fix the provenance of Royce's concept of *self* and to identify some problems associated with the Roycean account. He finds two
main sources: German idealism (especially Hegel) and
pragmatism (especially Peirce). The *primary* inspiration
is German idealism; the pragmatic elements, most notably
Peirce's theory of signs, are grafts. Most of Fuss's attention,
accordingly, is focused on Royce's relation to the post-
Kantian idealists—Fichte, Schelling, and, pre-eminently,
Hegel. Royce's historical writings, particularly *Lectures
on Modern Idealism* and *The Spirit of Modern Philosophy*, let us see him working with some of the philosophers
from whom he drew most heavily in developing his own
view of the self.

It was (as it seemed to them) the unfinished philosophy
of Kant that fired the imaginations of Fichte, Schelling,
and Hegel; nothing moved them more ineluctably toward
the notion of the absolute than the unresolved tensions
among Kant's three different selves—the empirical "me,"
the transcendental unity of apperception, and the rational
moral self. Kant's own self-imposed limitations regarding
the scope of human knowledge prevented him (or excused
him) from trying to synthesize the realm of scientific
knowledge (and the necessary conditions thereof) with
the world of moral action. His idealistic successors labored
under no such constraints.

Fichte and Schelling, in their different ways, introduced
the notion of the self as dialectical, as being *absolute* by
reason of implying or "containing" its other. But neither
of them was able to develop this insight into a coherent,
full-bodied doctrine. That task fell to Hegel, who managed
it with a thoroughness and subtlety befitting his genius.

Royce quite properly devotes more than one-third of
Lectures on Modern Idealism to Hegel, and he correctly
locates the supreme expression of Hegel's genius in *The*

Phenomenology of Mind. (Fuss has some illuminating remarks on the meaning and etymology of *Geist*, which is usually and misleadingly translated as "mind.") For Hegel the self—with its principle, consciousness—embodies an unrest, a congenital inability to be content with any determinate object, just as an object. It is in its very nature self-corrective and all-inclusive; because it "comprehends" (in the sense of *begreifen*) both its object and its own knowledge of that object, it annuls the Kantian bifurcation of reality into noumenal and phenomenal. Nothing is, or can be, ultimately foreign to the self; and that could not be true if nature were a lifeless substance expressible in mathematical equations. It is on this consideration that Hegel hangs his transformation of "substance" into "subject." By a double-edged dialectical move, Hegel deobjectifies substance/matter and depersonalizes self/subject, thereby making possible their interaction and unification.

All of this Royce understands, waveringly and intermittently. He sees clearly that, on Hegel's view, there is neither finite nor infinite as such, that is, as sundered from one another. The infinite has no existence apart from its finite expressions; it is "the totality of the finite viewed in its unity." For Hegel, then, we cannot locate the absolute, or God, outside ourselves. The absolute we seek is in the principle of selfhood, in the self's refusal to accept unresolved dualisms—in short, in its drive to all-inclusiveness.

Unfortunately, Royce's clear-eyed philosophical vision is a sometime thing; it is prone to become cloudy just when he is most in need of clarity. For example, he vacillates on the status of the absolute, repeatedly yielding to the temptation to hypostatize a transcendent, fixed Absolute (with a capital "A"), in obvious violation of some of his own astute expositions of Hegel. Given his distortion of Hegel's internal dialectic of consciousness into something external and reductionistic, it is hardly surprising that he cannot remain true to Hegel's insight. For various reasons, Royce continues to search for an absolute, all-inclusive subject after he has already found it in human selfhood and consciousness.

It was alleged earlier that the pragmatic elements in Royce's philosophy are grafts. *The Problem of Christianity*, Royce's last book and the fullest expression of his debt to Peirce, bears out this claim. The absolute to which Royce is now attracted is God qua "Infinite Interpreter." But essentially the same misunderstandings and half-understandings—the same mechanical use of dialectic and the same impulse to sever God from the human self—infect his account of the interpretational community as infected his earlier efforts.

Frederick A. Olafson's essay "George Santayana and the Idea of Philosophy" is about a man who had some hard things to say about America and American thought. There is, then, a certain condign irony in the fact that Santayana's own thinking is, to a significant extent, the product of his experience in America. Not least among the formative elements in his philosophy are the targets he chose for criticism—especially what seemed to him the anthropomorphic views typified by James and Royce. According to Santayana, these men (who expressed at a higher level the views of many other philosophers) lacked the cardinal virtue of a philosopher—disinterestedness, the force of mind needed to spurn the temptation to enlist the universe in support of our deepest moral and religious concerns. Though vastly more sophisticated than their fideistic counterparts in the churches, philosophers like James and Royce ultimately could not accept the plain fact that human beings are just physical organisms in a material world—or so Santayana sized up the views of his Harvard colleagues.

Putting aside the question whether Santayana's criticisms of philosophers like James and Royce are fair or accurate (Olafson has his doubts), Olafson turns to Santayana's own account of reason and its powers. That account ties reason closely to the material conditions on which it depends for its very existence; and Santayana never tires of chiding those who, in his opinion, forget that human rationality is a happy accident. (It is worth noting parenthetically that, for all his stress on the derivative and inefficacious character of consciousness, Santayana was not a reductive materialist. He was too fond of the life of the spirit for that.)

Olafson's chief complaint against Santayana's theory is not, as one might expect, that Santayana exempts his own philosophy from the stultifying consequences of the theory. It is, rather, that in emphasizing the lability of reason, Santayana tends to underestimate its legitimate authority. He seems not to realize that it is nothing against the internal autonomy of reason that it rests on natural conditions. Reason does indeed rest on a thousand natural conditions, but it does not therefore follow that rationality must be nothing but a transcription of some features of the natural order. And it does not follow, either, that we could read off the necessary structure of our rational processes from a more complete knowledge of our physical constitution. Precarious though it is, once reason appears in the world, philosophers owe it unconditional allegiance for the kind of possible life it represents. Reason has a normative status not reducible to mere impulse or force; indeed, the claims of "life" and "spontaneity" must be subject to the scrutiny of reason.

The strength and weakness of Santayana's approach are apparent in what many consider his greatest work,

The Life of Reason. We might even say that he has the weakness *of* his strength, and vice versa. Consider, for example, Santayana's treatment of religion. Some readers may be inclined to agree that the propositions of religion are not literally *about* anything and that religion itself is the product of an illicit union of moral imagination and a fantastic cosmology. But such a genetic explanation tells us precious little of the significance of religion in human history or in the life of an individual. Even if religious claims cannot be taken literally, and even if religion is ultimately symbolic, we cannot but think that Santayana's account is seriously truncated, that religion is richer and more complex as a form of human thought than Santayana realized. Santayana's myopic vision is even more evident in his handling of morality, if only because it is by no means obvious that moral statements *must* be expressive or symbolic in the way religious claims are.

It is Santayana's great virtue to see that reason has a natural habitat and that, consequently, the highfalutin pretensions of rationalist philosophers must be viewed with skepticism. However, it is a serious mistake to suppose, as Santayana does, that the authority of reason may not validly go beyond the natural conditions on which it depends. So long as it lives, reason is the master of the house—even though it may be suddenly and unceremoniously ejected.

In his essay "Facts of the Matter" W. V. Quine argues for an undogmatic, nonreductionist physicalism, justifying this ontology on (roughly) pragmatic grounds. But even this toned-down version of materialism does not get top billing: "Sentences, in their truth or falsity, are what run deep; ontology is by the way."

Why sentences? Well, for one important reason, sentences—or, rather, certain kinds of basic sentences—are not theoretical in the way all objects are. The basic type of sentence is what Quine calls *occasion* sentences—sentences whose truth or falsity changes from utterance to utterance, depending on the occasion; for example, 'It's raining', 'There goes a rabbit', 'This is red'. Those occasion sentences that get the highest marks for clarity (those that are most likely to be agreed upon by witnesses from occasion to occasion) are called *observation* sentences. Observation sentences are basic in language learning: they often are, and always could be, acquired directly by conditioning. They are sentences that we can learn without having to learn others first. Of course, much of language cannot be acquired in this simple inductive way, but all language rests, however tenuously, on this observational base. Observation sentences are also basic in science: it is through them that science acquires its empirical content, and it is to them that a scientist turns when he seeks to defend a disputed hypothesis.

Ontology becomes an issue only when we turn from sentences to terms and the objects to which the terms (putatively) refer. Ordinary language is too vague and untidy to help us decide which objects to admit into our ontology. Even to raise ontological questions in a way that admits of clear-cut answers, we require a regimented, object-oriented language. The language that Quine recommends is the classic predicate calculus, with its predicates, variables, quantifiers, and truth functions. Our ontology will comprise "just the objects that the variables of quantification admit as values."

The paradigmatic case of objects is bodies; bodies are first and foremost among the values of our variables. But if we aim to do science (or to reflect on what scientists do), we cannot get on with nothing but bodies. We must quantify over classes, numbers, and functions, and thereby add them to bodies as part of our ontology. In spite of this extension of our ontic commitments, we will, if we are physicalists, continue to regard bodies as fundamental in the following sense: "there is no change without a change in the positions or states of bodies."

What is a change in the position or state of a body—or what we may call, for short, a "physical difference"? The easy answers of Descartes, Hobbes, or even Dalton, have been undermined by an ever-multiplying swarm of so-called elementary particles; and even the utility of the particle model itself has been called into question. What we need, it seems, are regions of space-time to which various states, in varying degrees, may be directly ascribed. The space-time regions may be regarded as sets of space-time points, each of which is to be identified with a quadruple of real or complex numbers according to an arbitrary system of coordinates. And the real numbers, by which we measure the intensity of the various states, can be constructed in pure set theory—set theory stripped clean of concrete objects.

The "brave new ontology" that emerges—"the purely abstract ontology of pure set theory, pure mathematics"— would seem to be a physicalist's nightmare. Add to this the reflection that any consistent formal system may be interpreted in a number of ways, and the debacle is complete. Starting with an ontology of old-fashioned, dependable, solid bodies, we end with a kind of twentieth-century Pythagoreanism. We have arrived at what appears to be the *reductio ad absurdum* of physicalist ontology.

Where does all this leave physicalism? According to Quine, it leaves a properly formulated physicalism pretty much unaffected; but the reformulation must be in terms of physical vocabulary, not in terms of etherealized physical objects. As for the abstract entities, a right-thinking physicalist would not have demanded an *exclusively* corporeal ontology in any event; he would have regarded physical objects—however the details of their constitution may be filled in—as fundamental. The reformulated claim of physicalism is that "there is no difference in matters of fact without a difference in the fulfillment of the physical-state predicates by space-time regions." Discovering a minimum list of "elementary states" such that there is no change without a change in respect to them—this is the continuing task of physics. This brand of physicalism is not reductionistic in any strong sense: it does not assume that anyone be in a position to apply the appropriate physical-state predicate(s) in any particular case.

Let us now tie Quine's physicalism to his views on language. His well-known *Gedankenexperiment* in radical translation is not motivated by ontological considerations but rather by intractable problems with synonymy. (Some readers may object that Quine's difficulties with synonymy are the *result* of his commitment to physicalism and behaviorism. But that is an issue for the reader to decide.)

Consider the case of two translators of an initially unknown language, each of whom compiles a translation manual. Both manuals are consistent with all speech behavior and all dispositions to speech behavior; yet each translator rejects portions of the other's manual. What are we to say in this case? Utility and aesthetics aside, there is in this situation no fact of the matter that makes one translation right and the other wrong; or, to put it in the jargon of physicalism, "both manuals are compatible with the fulfillment of just the same elementary physical states by space-time regions." The criterion of correctness in radical translation is conformity to observed behavior; and where two different translations satisfy this criterion, there is no basis for preferring one to the other—especially since translators cannot (at present anyway) invoke neurological criteria or telepathy to supplement their behavioral criteria. The two translations do not, in other words, reflect different facts of the matter. Quine characterizes them as "different" only because each translator rejects parts of the other's manual.

Quine's physicalism now appears in a clear light. By contrast, a philosopher who admits propositions or meanings would have no trouble in saying how, even in the absence of behavioral differences, the two translation manuals differ and how one may be right and the other wrong; namely, they express different propositions or meanings. For such a philosopher there *is* a fact of the matter that can be invoked to settle the dispute. Of course, the two translators may be mistaken in believing the other to be wrong, but the point is that on this anti-Quinean view it makes sense to suppose a difference in meaning even when there is no physical difference. For Quine, there is no fact of the matter but what consists in physical states; and *this*, not the alleged reducibilfty of mental talk to physical talk, is the essential truth of behaviorism.

There is in all this nothing in the nature of a proof. That would be contrary to the spirit and the letter of Quine's undertaking. All ontologies are free creations. Are we, then, thrown back on nothing more substantial than personal preference? No, not really. For while all ontologies are free creations, they are not all created equal. Physicalism has the advantage over other ontologies of settling on objects that are, in some reasonably clear sense, publicly identifiable—a circumstance that provides an anchor for the system. A good conceptual scheme ought to aid in the discovery of causal explanations. By allying itself with physics, physicalism holds the best promise of meeting that requirement.

Beauty and Politics: A Problematic Legacy of Jonathan Edwards

Roland A. Delattre

I

Beauty and politics, as the title of a lecture on Jonathan Edwards, doubtless requires some explanation, since most people are not likely to associate either of these terms with him. We are approaching a time when it will no longer be necessary to demonstrate the formative place of beauty in Edwards' vision of reality, though it is necessary to review some of the ingredients in such a demonstration in so far as it bears upon my intention of exploring the relation of beauty to politics in Edwards' thought. That relationship exposes to view what I find most problematic in the Edwardsean legacy.

While the concept and experience of beauty are absolutely fundamental to Edwards' thought, he displays hardly any interest in politics or in the institutional arrangements and forms essential to political life. And yet his interpretation of the religious life and the Great Awakening, of which he was a major spokesman, exercised such an enormous influence upon the course of the American Revolution that some historians now portray the Revolution as in considerable measure a continuation of the religious revolution of the Awakening through political means—a political extension of the religious revolution set in motion by the Awakening. Furthermore, the political influence of Edwards continued to be felt among Americans through the tradition of revivalism and the benevolence movements of evangelical protestantism in the nineteenth century and also into the twentieth century. It is entirely appropriate that a small movement within and over against the bureaucratic structures of the *National Council of Churches,* impatient with what they found to be the sterility and complacence of the religious establishment and committed to radical spiritual renewal and political relevance amidst the struggles of the 1960's, should have called itself "Jonathan's Wake" and made its headquarters in Stockbridge, Massachusetts. That was the place to which Edwards had gone as a missionary to the Indians in 1751 in the wake of a dispute over the minimal terms of full church membership, an altercation that brought on his dismissal by the Northampton congregation he had served for over twenty years. We have reason to be grateful for the half dozen years he spent in Stockbridge, for they were his philosophically most productive ones.

The political legacy of Jonathan Edwards is problematic for reasons that are largely historical and also very complex. This is not the occasion for unraveling that complex history. Systematic rather than historical issues will be considered. But a few words should be said about the latter, because the two cannot be neatly separated and because it is the problematic character of that historical legacy that provides the occasion for my interest in returning behind that history to engage Edwards himself with regard to the relation of beauty to politics. The Great Awakening helped prepare the ground for the Revolution by challenging established patterns of local ecclesiastical authority and colonial political authority even as it contributed significantly to the development of intercolonial communication and unity. In addition, many who associated themselves with Edwards tended to espouse a more radically egalitarian, libertarian, and fraternal view of the religious life — and then also of the social and political life — than did their more socially conservative opponents, whether orthodox, liberal, or deist.

These and other considerable achievements were qualified in various ways by the fact that even his closest followers never fully shared or appropriated unto themselves his conviction that in the experience of beauty we are given the most critical disclosure of the nature of reality. The manner of God's governance, which for Edwards if by the attractive power or beauty of the apparent good, continues to be understood by his followers in conventional deontological and moralistic terms. One sees this skewing of the political legacy at work even among great figures in whom there is otherwise much to be grateful for — as in Samuel Hopkins, who was moved by his Edwardsean convictions to preach against slavery from his pulpit in Newport itself long before others took up the issue as important; and in Isaac Backus, as he deployed Edwardsean rhetoric in his arguments for religious liberty before and after the Revolution. In the evangelical tradition of revivalism the name of Edwards is praised while the emotional and affectional life is cut off from the life of reason, and religion becomes a private matter of inward piety informing only in the most indirect and generally unconstructive ways the wider social and political structures and institutions. Where this tradition has not been privatistic in its conception of the religious life, it has been moralistic and sometimes lent itself to the most arrogant cultural and political imperialism in the name of a presumed identity between God's redemptive activity in history and the purposes of the new Republic — God's New Israel. Such developments are a mark of the distance from Edwards' vision traveled by many who invoke his name.

If we are to identify an alternative and less problematic political legacy from Jonathan Edwards, we must start again with the concept of beauty which was at the center of what is most fundamental and distinctive to the Edwardsean vision of reality. Only since the pioneering work of H. Richard Niebuhr and Perry Miller has this aspect of the Edwardsean legacy begun to find willing heirs. One of the fruits of this reassessment is a revision of the received wisdom of our culture about the relation of Edwards to other American philosophers and theologians. William Clebsch, for example, has recently portrayed Emerson and William James as the principal heirs and contributors to an American tradition of "aesthetic spirituality" inaugurated by Edwards. My own reading of him would—if time permitted our telling the story— revise that judgment to the extent at least of placing Edwards in as significant a companionship with Thoreau as with Emerson, and as close to Royce as to James. What I propose is simply that we take seriously Edwards' frequent and crucially located declarations that the experience and concept of beauty are central to his whole vision of reality, and that we explore the political implications and resonances of that conviction, following out its logic and its harmonics.

II

It is essential to an understanding of Edwards' thought that we have clearly in view his conception of beauty, for, though it is not eccentric, it does extend somewhat our ordinary usage of the term. He distinguishes two principal kinds of beauty. The kind that comes most readily to mind consists in some variation upon what can be summarily expressed in terms of the concepts of harmony and proportion. To Edwards the beauty of harmony and proportion is real and of sufficient spiritual significance that, for example, he lists "beautiful symmetry and proportion" as the tenth of his twelve signs that religious affections are truly gracious and holy [RA 365]. But he calls this sort of beauty merely secondary or natural, for he finds in it but an image of another and higher form of beauty which he calls primary or spiritual beauty, and which consists in being's cordial or affectional consent to being in general.

A useful and more expansive formulation of this contrast between primary and secondary beauty appears in chapter three of the dissertation *The Nature of True Virtue,* the first chapter of which had opened with the confident declaration that, however widely opinion may vary about the nature of virtue, everyone seriously concerned about the subject means by it "something beautiful, or rather some kind of beauty or excellency" [TV 1]. The issue is simply what *kind* of beauty, and the principal options are distinguished as follows:

> That consent, agreement, or union of being to being which has been spoken of [in the opening two chapters on the true beauty of moral agents], viz. the union or propensity of minds to mental or spiritual existence, may be called the highest and *primary beauty;* being the proper and peculiar beauty of spiritual and moral beings, which are the highest and first part of the universal system, for whose sake all the rest has existence. Yet there is another, inferior, *secondary beauty,* which is some image of this, and which is not peculiar to spiritual beings, but is found even in inanimate things; which consists in a mutual consent and agreement of different things, in form, manner, quantity, and visible end or design; called by the various names of regularity, order, uniformity, symmetry, proportion, harmony, etc. . . . [including] uniformity in the midst of variety [TV 27–28; italics added].

What is common to both kinds of beauty is consent; each is a variety of the single rule of beauty as "agreement or consent" as opposed to "discord and dissent." What distinguishes primary from secondary beauty is that "the will, disposition, and affections of the heart" are involved in the consent:

> there are two sorts of agreement or consent of one thing to another. (1) There is a *cordial* agreement; that consists in concord and union of mind and heart: which, if not attended (viewing things in general) with more discord than concord, is . . . primary beauty . . . . (2) There is a *natural* union or agreement; which, though some image of the other, is entirely a distinct thing; the will, disposition, or affection of the heart having no concern in it, but consisting only in uniformity and consent of nature, form, quantity, etc. (as before described), wherein lies an inferior secondary sort of beauty, which may in distinction from the other, be called natural beauty [TV 31–32; italics added].

The object of consent is as essential to the definition of beauty as is the character of the consenting being. In the case of primary or spiritual beauty, that object must be either other minds or other things. If the consent be "of minds towards minds," says Edwards, "it is love, and when of minds towards other things, it is choice" [Mind 45]. Love and choice, then, are forms of consent and beauty. We shall have occasion to find in this statement from Edwards' youthful "Notes on the Mind" a convenient way of formulating the unity of his thought, at least in its essential features, and finding the same aesthetically articulated system of thought in his treatise *Freedom of the Will* as in *Religious Affections.* But first there are a few additional general observations to make about his conception of beauty.

The significance of beauty for Edwards' systematically developed vision of reality is difficult to overstate. The case can and needs to be put both philosophically and theologically. The theological position can be stated in a couple of sentences and left for further development below. Central to the Edwardsean theology is his conviction that

God is God, and distinguished from all other beings, and exalted above 'em, chiefly by his divine beauty, which is infinitely diverse from all other beauty. They therefore that see the stamp of this glory in divine things, they see divinity in them, they see God in them, and so see 'em to be divine; because they see that in them wherein the truest idea of divinity does consist [RA 298].

As I have sought to show at some length in my book on Edwards,* the distinguishing mark of his theology, when looked at in relation to the whole history of Christian thought, is his radical elevation of beauty to pre-eminence among the divine perfections.

The philosophical version of this position can be briefly stated. In any genuinely systematic philosophy, the character of the entire enterprise is shaped in a decisive way by the first move that is made in its development. Edwards' philosophy is a philosophy of being, and his first move in the articulation of that philosophy is to establish beauty as the first principle of being and the central category in terms of which to interpret that system of being. "Examined narrowly," he observes in his "Notes on the Mind," being "is nothing but proportion" [Mind 1]. Examined more widely, being as such consents to being, "being or existence is what is necessarily agreeable to being" [Mind 62]. Beauty is the first principle of being, the power of being by virtue of which and by participation in which all that is stands out from nonentity or "nothing." Because beauty has its own distinctive manner of articulation, the character of the whole system of being is decisively marked

*Editors' note: The book to which Professor Delattre refers is *Beauty and Sensibility in the Thought of Jonathan Edwards* (New Haven, Yale University Press, 1968).

by the ontological priority of beauty as the first and formative principle of being.

Edwards' conception of beauty is objective and structural. This does not mean that beauty is simply in the object, as though that were the only alternative to the subjectivist and relativist theories of beauty—according to which beauty is only in the eye of the beholder. Rather, beauty is objective because it is constituted by objective relations of consent and dissent among beings, relations into which the subject or beholder may enter and participate, but relations the beauty of which is defined primarily by affectional and active consent to being rather than by the degree of subjective pleasure. Beauty is, for Edwards, a structural concept, the nearest synonym for which is excellence or intrinsic validity, rather than pleasantness.

Although beauty is objectively defined by the relation of being to being, it is a paradigm of that kind of order which cannot be apprehended apart from or without being enjoyed—that is, without an affectional response of the subject. Indeed, appearance to perceiving, enjoying being is essential to the very being of beauty. To conceive of beauty as the first principle of being is, therefore, a way of systematically construing being itself as inclined to disclose and communicate itself. This, too, is one of the ways in which the characteristics of beauty inform the manner in which the Edwardsean system of being is articulated.

III

Jonathan Edwards is widely known, particularly among philosophers—and justly so—for the energy and intelligence with which he contested every theological or philosophical position which in any way qualified or pretended to qualify the absolute sovereignty of God. What is less widely known or understood is that, according to Edwards, God exercises that sovereign power by governing his intelligent perceiving creatures primarily through the attractive and creative and re-creative power of his own beauty, rather than by his terrifying power to reward and punish and to force the course of events in nature and history to conform to his will. Since Edwards sought to understand all things in relation to God, it is precisely in the pattern of divine governance that we can expect to find the essential features of an Edwardsean political philosophy respecting the governance of human affairs.

In Edwards' view, not only the moral, but also the natural world is governed in accordance with the divine beauty. And we may begin with the natural world by observing that for Edwards the secondary beauty of harmony and proportion is the first law of the natural world. In one of his "Miscellanies" on "God's Moral Government" he finds that there is

much evidence of the most perfect exactness of proportion harmony equity & beauty in the mechanical laws of nature & other methods of providence which belong to the course of nature which are means by which God shews his regard to harmony fitness and beauty in what he does as the Governour of the natural world [Misc. 1196].

It is the specific operations and relations of the corporeal, material, natural world that Edwards has in mind when he finds it governed according to the secondary beauty of proportion and harmony. In *Images or Shadows of Divine Things* he observes:

The whole material universe is preserved by gravity or attraction, or the mutual tendency of all bodies to each other. One part of the universe is hereby made beneficial to another; the beauty, harmony, and order, regular progress, life, and motion, and in short all the well-being of the whole frame depends on it [Images 79].

Both the being and the well-being of the material universe depend upon the operation of the first law of the natural world.

That world's secondary beauty is also an expression of the instrumental and dependent relation of the natural to the moral world, according to which the beauty of the former consists in its shadowing forth the beauty of the latter. "The moral world is the end of the natural world" [FW 251], and "the beauty of the corporeal world consists chiefly in its imaging forth spiritual beauties" [Misc. 186]. So much so that, although for Edwards "there is no proper consent but that of minds" [Mind 45], he sometimes speaks of natural as well as spiritual beauty in terms of consent— as in another passage in *Images:*

The beauty of the world consists wholly of sweet mutual consents, either within itself or with the supreme being. As to the corporeal world, though there are many other sorts of consents, yet the sweetest and most charming beauty of it is its resemblance of spiritual beauties. The reason is that spiritual beauties are infinitely the greatest, and bodies being but the shadows of beings, they must be so much the more charming as they shadow forth spiritual beauties [Images, p. 135].

Accordingly, although the beauty of the natural world is real and substantial, and its relation to the even more substantial beauty of the spiritual world is typological rather than metaphorical, nonetheless the beauty that is the law of the natural world is but the shadow of the beauty by which the spiritual world is governed. And it is the manner of the divine governance of this world of intelligent, perceiving beings that most concerns us here.

One way to clarify how beauty, which is for Edwards the first principle of order in the whole system of being, is also the principle of political order, is to consider his famous proposition about the will: "The will always is as the greatest apparent good is" [FW 142]. Unlike the defini-

tions of the will offered by some of Edwards' opponents
in the controversy that occasioned the publication of his
Freedom of the Will, this is a descriptive rather than a
causal account of the will—and it must be remembered
that for Edwards the will is not a faculty of the self, but
rather it is a way of speaking about the self as a whole in
its affectional engagement with reality as good and evil,
pleasing and not, attractive and not. Edwards rejects as
an "absurd and inconsistent notion" the idea that the essence of the moral good or evil of the will "lies not in
their nature, but in their cause" [FW 341].

'Tis a certain beauty or deformity that are *inherent* in that
good or evil will, which is the *soul* of virtue and vice (and not
in the *occasion* of it) which is their worthiness of esteem or
disesteem, praise or dispraise, according to the common sense
of mankind [FW 340; italics are Edwards'].

He does not say that the will is determined by the apparent good or by anything else besides its own pleasure,
but that it *is as* the greatest apparent good is. The will is
neither autonomously indeterminate nor heteronomously
determined by something outside itself. Rather, the will
is in correspondence with its object, the apparent good.

The critical passage is the following one from the early
pages of *Freedom of the Will:*

I have rather chosen to express myself thus, that the will *is*
as the greatest apparent good, or as what appears most agreeable
is, than to say that the will is *determined* by the greatest apparent
good, or by what seems most agreeable; because an appearing
most agreeable or pleasing to the mind, and the mind's preferring and choosing, seem hardly to be properly and perfectly
distinct [FW 144; italics Edwards'].

They are not distinct; to speak of one is but to speak of the
other in a different way. Even when he does use the language of determination, it is clear that what is offered
is a descriptive rather than a causal account, because both

sides of the volitional equation figure in the determination of what it is that will appear good or agreeable. "If strict propriety of speech be insisted on," he says later on the same page just quoted,

it may more properly be said . . . that the act of volition itself is always determined by that in or about the mind's view of the object, which causes it to appear most agreeable. I say, in or about the mind's view of the object, because what has influence to render an object in view agreeable, is not only what appears in the object viewed, but also the manner of the view, and the state and circumstances of the mind that views [FW 144].

The greatest apparent good cannot be said to stand in a causal relation to the will if the very being of that good *as apparent* good is in some measure a function of the affectional disposition or spiritual condition of the perceiving, enjoying self. And the relation of descriptive correspondence is not peculiar to the pages of the treatise *Freedom of the Will*. Variations on that theme occur throughout Edwards' writings, as in the *Religious Affections,* where he observes that people "show the differences of their natures"—that is, the conditions of their wills—"very much in the different things they relish as their proper good, one delighting in that which another abhors" [RA 262]. Much of what needs to be observed about beauty as the first article in the constitution of the moral (as well as the natural) world is contained in this "is as" volitional equation.

In the first place, and at the risk of insisting too much upon the obvious, it is clear that "apparent good" is a synonym for "beauty." Edwards does not say that the will is as the greatest good is, but as the greatest *apparent* good is. Beauty is the good become apparent, the good as immediately agreeable and attractive. Beauty is the attractive power of the good. As he says in *The Nature of True Virtue,* that form or quality is called beautiful, which appears in itself agreeable or comely, or the view of which is immediately pleasant to the mind. . . . Indirect agreeableness or eligibleness in things not for themselves, but for something else, is not beauty. But when a form or quality appears lovely, pleasing and delightful in itself, then it is called beautiful; and this agreeableness or gratefulness of the idea is beauty [TV 98].

It is, accordingly, by a direct sensation or immediate experience of the beauty or deformity in the object that anything becomes to the self its greatest apparent good or evil. And one can, on Edwards' view, determine or measure the moral or spiritual quality of the will by attending to the nature and quality of the beauty which the will is as. Is it the primary beauty of being's cordial consent to being in general? The secondary beauty of harmony and proportion? The limited and partial beauty of consent to and harmony with only a private or confined realm of being? Or perhaps it is a false beauty that is really, on a wider view of things, a deformity, for it stands in dissent against a larger good and a wider realm of being.

In the second place, the good in question in the "is as" volitional equation is apparent immediately, rather than by either argument or speculation. As Edwards observes in one of the "Notes" that contributed to the preparation of *Freedom of the Will:*

Merely the rationally judging that a thing is lovely in itself, without a sensibleness of the beauty and pleasantness of it, signifies nothing towards influencing the will . . . . Therefore, if a man has only a rational judgment that a thing is beautiful and lovely, without any sensibleness of the beauty . . . he will never choose it [Misc. 436].

Edwards then goes on to argue in that note that such a sense of the beauty of the object, if it is in fact a lively sense, will prevail in the determination of the will even over a rational judgment to the contrary. The role of beauty in this determination of choice can also be expressed in terms of love (that other term for speaking about the will or the self as moral agent). To love is to be attracted to something as good, and in Edwards' view "all love arises from a perception, either of consent to being-in-general or a consent to that being that perceives" [Misc. 117].

This raises, in the third place, an important and interesting problem with political implications to which Edwards addresses himself in *The Nature of True Virtue,* where he shows that beauty is the secondary rather than the primary ground of virtuous love or a truly good will. He distinguishes between two kinds of love, benevolence and complacence. Benevolence is an active, affectional attachment to and delight in the well-being and happiness of others simply as being, without presupposing any beauty in them. Complacence, on the other hand, presupposes beauty in the object and "is no other than delight in beauty" [TV 6].

The problem is this: "If virtue be the beauty of an intelligent being, and virtue consists in love, then it is a plain inconsistency to suppose that virtue primarily consists in any love to its object for its beauty" [TV 6]. "For that would be to suppose that the beauty of intelligent beings primarily consists in the love of beauty," in which case beauty, the thing loved, must also consist in the love of beauty, so that virtue would consist in the love of the love of beauty, "and so on in infinitum" [TV 7]. But virtue is not prior to itself any more than the apparent good is causally prior to the condition of the will in the "is as" volitional equation.

Therefore, if the essence of virtue, or beauty of mind, lies in love, or a disposition to love, it must primarily consist in something different both from complacence, which is a delight in

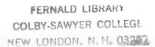

beauty, and also from any benevolence that has the beauty of its object for its foundation [TV 7].

That "something different" which is "the first object of a [truly] virtuous benevolence is being, simply considered" [TV 8]. Accordingly, true virtue—whether exercised in private or public, in personal or political life—"most essentially consists in *benevolence to being in general.* Or . . . it is that consent, propensity and union of heart to being in general, which is immediately exercised in a general good will" [TV 3; italics Edwards']. But beauty enters as a secondary ground or object of virtuous benevolence because "loving a being on this ground necessarily arises from a pure benevolence to being in general, and *comes to the same thing* . . . . A spirit of consent to being must agree with consent to being" [TV 10; italics added].

It is critical to the operation and application of Edwards' theory that the love of beauty in being comes to the same thing in practice as the love of being. For one thing, no one ever has being in general, but always only a small part of the whole system of being for his direct and immediate object. Since every particular being or finite system of beings is encountered as standing in some relationship of consent and dissent, harmony and disharmony, rather than of indifference toward other beings and toward being-in-general, this means that being always presents itself to us in some determinate form of beauty or deformity. Furthermore, since no one act of human beings can have being in general as its direct and immediate object, its apparent good, Edwards finds that virtue consists essentially in dispositions rather than individual acts. "True virtue consists in a disposition to benevolence towards being in general; though from such a disposition may arise exercises of love to particular beings, as objects are presented and occasions arise" [TV 5]. Settled dispositions, not momentary visions or occasional acts, are what count.

The unity of Edwards' analysis in *Freedom of the Will* with that offered in *Religious Affections* needs to be stressed, for some interpreters of Edwards have been wont to find a different mind at work in the two treatises. The essential formulations in *Religous Affections* are identical with the pattern of the "is as" volitional equation in their portrayal of the manner of God's governance and redemption of the moral world through the attractive power of his own beauty. The subject there is the "affections of the mind" (as distinguished from the passions of the body), by which Edwards means "the more vigorous and sensible exercises of the inclination and will of the soul" [RA 96]. The focus is more upon the "will" than upon the "apparent good" side of the volitional equation, more upon the activity of the affections than upon the attractive power of the apparent good. But the same correspondences obtain as in *Freedom of the Will,* and the essential objectivism of Edwards' conception of beauty and of its authority as the law of the moral world is greatly insisted upon. The critical passages are the summary statements of the second and third of his twelve signs by which true religious affections are distinguished from false ones. According to the second sign, "the first objective ground of gracious affections, is the transcendently excellent and amiable nature of divine things, as they are in themselves; and not any conceived relation they bear to self, or self-interest" [RA 240]. Since "excellence" and "beauty" are virtually synonymous for Edwards, we might rephrase that in the form of the volitional equation: gracious affections (in the will) *are as* the beauty of their divine object is. Edwards himself seems to be tightening up his own formulation when he summarizes the third sign:

Those affections that are truly holy, are primarily founded on
the loveliness of the moral excellency of divine things. Or (to
express it otherwise), a love to divine things for the beauty and
sweetness of their moral excellency, is the first beginning and
spring of all holy affections [RA 253f.].

In the discussion of that third sign, Edwards points out
that nothing less than a manifestation and communication
of the divine beauty itself has the creative, transforming,
spiritual power sufficient to the reconciliation of the sin-
ner with God.

A sight of the awful greatness of God, may overpower men's
strength, and be more than they can endure; but if the moral
beauty of God be hid, the enmity of the heart will remain in
its full strength, no love will be enkindled, all will not be ef-
fectual to gain the will, but that will remain inflexible [RA 264f.].

He is critical, therefore, of some fellow participants in the
Great Awakening for putting "too much weight . . . on
discoveries of God's greatness, awful majesty, and natural
perfection . . . without any real view of the holy, lovely
majesty of God" [RA 265].

There are, in addition to the "is as" volitional equation,
two other formulations of divine governance which provide the raw materials for an Edwardsean theory of human
governance—to which I turn now for briefer consideration. One is the concept of consent, more widely employed
as a political than as an aesthetic concept, and certainly
essential to any political philosophy for this Republic.
The other is the vision of reality developed in the dissertation *Concerning the End for Which God Created
the World*.

IV

One of the things that makes the Edwardsean political
legacy so problematic is that, although it is possible to
develop an explicitly political theory out of his conception

of beauty, he himself gives us only a social and a religious but not a genuinely political development of the idea of consent. He writes, for example, of the primary beauty exhibited in "the consent of mind, of the different members of a society or system of intelligent beings, sweetly united in a benevolent agreement of heart" [TV 31], and he envisages a grander beauty than is manifest in personal virtue and the holiness of individuals—a social manifestation of spiritual beauty embodied in the constitution of genuine community among people. His postmillennial reading of history disposes him to look for anticipations of the heavenly city on earth, beginning perhaps in New England. "All the world shall then be as one church, one orderly, regular, beautiful society" [WR 493]. It will be

a time wherein the whole earth shall be united as one holy city, one heavenly family, men of all nations shall as it were dwell together, and sweetly correspond one with another, as brethren and children of the same father . . . a time wherein this whole great society shall appear in glorious beauty, in genuine amiable Christianity, and excellent order, as *a city compacted together, the perfection of beauty, an external excellency* shining with a reflection of the glory of Jehovah *risen upon it*, which shall be attractive and ravishing to all kings and nations [HA 446; italics in original].

The lessons he draws from the reflections upon the social manifestations of beauty tend always to resolve or sublimate political into social or familial or religious terms, as in the following passage from his published response in 1747 to a proposal by some ministers in Scotland that the churches on both sides of the Atlantic unite in a "concert of prayer" for yet further outpourings of the Holy Spirit.

How condecent, how beautiful, and of good tendency would it be, for multitudes of Christians, in various parts of the world,

by explicit agreement, to unite in such prayer as is proposed
to us.

Union is one of the most amiable things that pertains to human
society; yea, it is one of the most beautiful and happy things
on earth, which indeed makes earth most like heaven. God has
made of one blood all nations of men to dwell on the face of the
earth; hereby teaching us this moral lesson, that it becomes
mankind all to be united as one family. . . . A civil union, or a
harmonious agreement among men in the management of their
secular concerns, is amiable; but much more a pious union and
sweet agreement in the great business for which man was created,
and had power given him beyond the brutes; even the business
of religion; the life and soul of which is love. Union is spoken
of in Scripture as the peculiar beauty of the church of Christ. . . .
As it is the glory of the church of Christ that in all her members,
however dispersed, she is thus one, one holy society, one family,
one body; so it is highly desirable that this union should be
manifested, and become visible [HA 462f.].

It is clear from passages such as this that we shall have
to go beyond anything explicitly offered by Edwards if
we are to add to these social, familial, and religious versions of "being's cordial consent to being" a specifically
political conception.

Edwards himself gives us very little help and, at best,
comes just short of an explicitly political development
of his own analysis of human affairs. In *The Nature of
True Virtue* he discusses justice briefly, finding in it essentially a natural or secondary beauty of proportion,
and affirming that "benevolence to being in general will
naturally incline to justice" [TV 38]. He also suggests that
"just affections and acts have a beauty in them" that is in
some measure an expression of primary beauty as well as
an agreement with the will and command of God, "so that
the tendency of general benevolence to produce justice,
also the tendency of justice to produce effects agreeable
to general benevolence, both render justice pleasing to
a virtuous mind" [TV 38]. There the discussion fades

away, with only the parting thought that perhaps there may be some other beauty in justice—but without exploring the possibility and without ever considering justice as an essentially political virtue.

To develop a political theory out of his conception of beauty as being's cordial consent to being we need, then, to draw out the Edwardsean lines of thought beyond the point to which he develops them himself. One such line, taking as its point of departure the political resonances of the concept of consent, and proceeding in the same Edwardsean spirit as is displayed in *The Nature of True Virtue,* might be developed as follows.

Political order, like the personal order of virtue, is properly to be imagined as a kind of beauty; and the moral or spiritual condition of the political order is as the beauty of its greatest apparent good is. The political order is a symbolic universe of human action and discourse which may properly be said to come into being as people commit themselves to the intrinsic validity or beauty of the plurality of human being. Politics comes into being and is sustained in being, essentially, by the affectional consent of human beings to the plurality of human being. Politics is the activity through which human beings exercise together, by mutual or common consent, their governance over that portion of reality marked by human presence. The mutual consent may be for the most part only implicitly rather than explicitly given, but it must not be any less deliberately given. If consent is exercised through the machinery of political agency or representation, continuing participation in politics remains nevertheless an essential condition if politics is not to give way to some other mode of governance over the public realm—administrative or authoritarian or familial, for example. Politics is decisive for human being, not because it properly embraces all other public activities, but because it is the arena

in which human beings resolve collectively — by deliber-
ation or by default — what will be the quality, order, shape,
and appearance of things so far as they reflect human
presence in the world. Politics is the symbolic space into
which the most fundamental tensions within and between
societies are brought or make their appearance, hopefully
for resolution — if not by consent, then by violence, and if
by violence, then by the dissolution of politics.

Political freedom is the freedom to do as one pleases.
It is more than an inward or private freedom of thought,
but requires that there be no arbitrary fracturing of the
correspondence between the will and its greatest apparent
good. Political freedom comes into being where the liberty
of movement and freedom of action in which that correspondence is actualized is not infringed by arbitrary authority. Just as God governs according to his pleasure,
and his freedom consists in his being pleased only with
beauty in being, so the measure of political freedom will
be the spiritual beauty and deformity of the realities (and
illusions) in which our pleasure is taken.

To interpret politics in terms of beauty and the cordial
consent of being to being does not require us to obscure
in the least the conflictual character of politics. Consent
to being in general or to the plurality of human being
may call for dissent in word and deed against those who
stand in a dissenting or destructive relation to those realities. Dissent from particular human beings and movements will be required, not on the grounds that they are
out of harmony or in disagreement with me, but only
where and when they are destructive of other beings and
of the wider system of being — and particularly in so far
as they are destructive of genuine human plurality and
dissent from its beauty. Just as beauty in being is enhanced
by dissent from dissenting being, so the beauty of human
plurality — and hence the reality of the political order —

is served by dissent from human beings in so far as they dissent from the beauty of human plurality.

No model of order—certainly none offered by Edwards—can promise to dissolve the conflictual elements in life. Even though the resolution of tension is involved in both beauty and politics, that resolution is not achieved by the dissolution of the various aesthetic or political ingredients into a bland and undifferentiated unity. It is achieved in politics by an overriding consent to each other's being among persons and agents who remain diverse, rather than by conformity of all parties to a single norm. Without genuine diversity and plurality there can be no beauty; the same is true of politics.

On the one hand, politics is relativized from an Edwardsean perspective. The most fundamental action runs deeper. On the other hand, there is built into that perspective a sense that since the plurality of human being is real and is also set within a wider fabric of relations extending throughout the whole system of being, it is humanly important to preserve the political order in its integrity as the arena in which the beauty of human plurality can appear and be celebrated, and as a realm in which human responsibility for the manner of our consent to yet wider systems of being—ecological, cosmological, and theological—is shared.

V

A work of Edwards' which I have not yet discussed, and which contributes significantly to such a wider rendering of the context within which the relativized political order is to be envisaged, is the dissertation *Concerning the End for Which God Created the World,* which I shall refer to hereafter as *End in Creation.* If we seek to share Edwards' perspective on reality, it may be worth noting what things seem to stand close together in his mind. I don't want to make too much of it, but consider the following. In 1738 Edwards delivered a series of sixteen lectures to his congregation on *Charity and its Fruits,* which he followed very soon with an even longer series on *The Work of Redemption.* Neither of these series of lectures was published in his lifetime. When he died twenty years later, he left ready for the press a pair of essays evidently intended for publication together, the dissertations *End in Creation* and *The Nature of True Virtue.*

It seems very likely that the themes of the two series of lectures—on love and redemption—were both on his mind during a considerable period of time, just as were the two dissertations at a later date. *The Nature of True Virtue* represents a dramatic recasting of his treatment of the subject of the earlier lectures, with love now interpreted systematically in terms of beauty—in addition, of course, to its being a highly sophisticated philosophical treatment of the theme explored in a more popular way in the earlier lectures. It may not be entirely fanciful, therefore, to see in the *End in Creation* a comparable and corresponding revision of the Edwardsean perspective on the work of redemption as embodied in the earlier lectures. If so, then it may also be possible to render less problematic the Edwardsean political legacy. The lectures on *The Work of Redemption* were published in various versions and circulated widely among evangelical Protestants for decades beginning in the mid-1770's. They lend support to what was already a powerful tendency among those who invoked Edwards' name—a tendency to identify the work of redemption closely with the founding of the new Republic, and to see in that political development a new stage in the advancement of the work of redemption. What I want to suggest is that *End in Creation* offers an alternative rendering of the context within which the political order is to be envisaged. It is not only to be read as a companion essay to *The Nature of True Virtue,* informed throughout by the same aesthetic vision of order as the latter. It is also to be read as a more metaphysical and aesthetic revision of the historical structure and dynamics of redemption as portrayed in the earlier lectures on the history of *The Work of Redemption.* The difference for the relation of beauty to politics is considerable and offers at least one way of reclaiming from Edwards himself a less problematic political legacy than the one that was claimed and passed on by most of those who in America have honored his name.

There is only one ultimate end for which God created the world, and that is summed up by Edwards as "the emanation and true external expression of God's internal glory and fulness" [EC 253]. That internal glory or fullness is itself complex or plural, consisting in three things: the glory or fullness of God's understanding, which is his infinite knowledge; of his will, which is his infinite virtue or holiness; and of his infinite joy or happiness. Edwards proceeds to resolve all of the other divine perfections—his power, infinity, eternity, immutability, and so on—into these three: his knowledge, his virtue or holiness, and his joy or happiness. Pre-eminent among these three is virtue or holiness, which "is in a peculiar manner the beauty of the divine nature," rendering "all his other attributes glorious and lovely" [RA 257].

"The external glory of God consists in a communication of these" three things to his intelligent, perceiving, and enjoying or willing creatures, in whom the image of God is displayed by their "knowing God's excellency, loving God for it, and rejoicing in it" [EC 254]. Once again, the pre-eminence of beauty in the Edwardsean vision of reality is manifest in that the knowledge thus communicated is of the excellency or beauty of God and then of all things in God; and the love is a participation in the divine benevolence to being in general, or primary beauty; while the joy is a participation in the divine complacence or delight in that same being and beauty—all of which is the subject of extended analysis in *The Nature of True Virtue*.

That, in sum, is the end for which God created the world, in the portrayal of which Edwards employs the imagery of light shining forth and of God as an over-flowing fountain of being and beauty, culminating in a sort of cosmic ecstasy:

In the creature's knowing, esteeming, loving, rejoicing in, and praising God, the glory of God is both *exhibited* and *acknowledged;* his fulness is received and returned. Here is both an *emanation* and *remanation*. The refulgence shines upon and into the creature, and is reflected back to the luminary. The beams of glory come from God, are something of God, and are refunded back again to their original. So that the whole is *of* God, and *in* God, and *to* God; and he is the beginning, and the middle, and the end in this affair [EC 255].

Since it is all one affair, Edwards finds in this pattern of divine activity in creation also the pattern of God's governance and redemption. Accordingly, the divine beauty or "the glory of God is the last end in his government of the world . . . and particularly in the work of redemption, the chief of all his dispensations in his moral government of the world" [EC 234]. Furthermore, he is confident that if God is to accomplish that great end in the creation and re-creation of the world "it will undoubtedly be by way of immediate emanation from his beauty" [Misc. 187].

As the reference to "dispensations" indicates, Edwards has not abandoned his intention to take up again the project begun in the lectures on *The Work of Redemption* and to write "in an entire new method" a theology "thrown into the form of a history" [FJ 411]. But in *End in Creation* he unfolds to view a vast system of being and beauty flowing forth from and remanating toward God, in which beauty is the pre-eminent mark of the divine presence in all things, and to which the appropriate human response is to participate in that beauty, glorifying God and enjoying him forever, by taking up a life in which that same beauty is exhibited to the world and reflected back to its source.

Now, however mystical this scheme may sound, it represents a shift in the fundamental rhythms of reality within which the movement of history is set—a shift with profound implications for our conception of politics. The logic of this vision of reality is to relativize the claim that the political order is to be understood religiously as the scene for a movement through history towards the kingdom of God. Edwards certainly envisages life on earth as essentially a pilgrimage toward that kingdom, and he was a postmillennialist who saw history in its final stage as a building up of that kingdom. But politics itself was less important to his conception of that enterprise than religion, and the state less important than the church. Perhaps this helps to explain why it is that the aesthetic dimensions of Edwards' thought became so marginal—or were transmuted into moral terms—among those who, in the Revolutionary period and on into the nineteenth century, brought to politics an otherwise Edwardsean perspective.

Edwards understood history teleologically, but in *End in Creation* we see most dramatically that in his conception of the telos of history the kingdom of God is taken up into the beauty and glory of God as both alpha and omega in the affair, and the governance of God over the creation is exercised less by establishing his authority than it is by communicating his beauty with such attractive power as to engender in the creature an answering and beautifying response of cordial consent to being. Indeed, the whole creation and its beauty—both primary and secondary—is extensively portrayed by Edwards as having a part in that solicitation. An Edwardsean approach to politics relativizes the politics of the Kingdom in these ways, without scorning teleologically oriented politics, by focusing attention less upon visions of some future ideal state of affairs than upon responsive and responsible experience of present realities in all their grades of beauty and deformity.

It is instructive to read *End in Creation* and *The Nature of True Virtue* as companion essays, for we can see that an Edwardsean political philosophy would need to bear the same relation to the former as does the analysis of personal virtue to the latter. Much remains to be done if we would lay claim to such an Edwardsean political legacy. What I have sought to do is to locate the aesthetic foundations for such an enterprise.

To build on those foundations, certain questions would have to be asked. What would be the quality of political life for one captivated by the divine beauty, caught up in the rhythms of a reality constituted by the ontological priority of beauty? What does it mean to occupy a political space in a symbolic universe so aesthetically constituted? What is the political meaning of setting the great deontological questions of right and wrong and the great teleological questions of good and evil within a moral context shaped by the priority of questions about beauty and deformity, of consent and dissent to being? Can the concept of beauty be made as descriptively and analytically illuminating of political reality as it is in Edwards' own deployment of it in his analysis of the full range of the religious life and of personal morality, where it serves him so well—not simply as a term of high praise and celebration, but as a structural and analytical resource for interpreting the deformities of sin no less than the beauties of virtue, and everything in between?

Although their resonances would need to be sounded out, some convictions would be fundamental: Where the plurality of human being and the importance of a symbolic and physical public space in which such plurality can make its appearance is not affirmed and celebrated as beautiful, as intrinsically good and beautiful rather than merely as an instrumental good, then politics dissolves into some other mode of governance—administrative or bureaucratic, authoritarian or totalitarian, familial or tribal, perhaps, but not political. The constitution of a genuinely political order is a humanly crucial expression of a radically monotheistic commitment and of cordial consent to the being and the beauty and the beautification of the wider orders of reality within which the modest scope of human responsibility is set. The fundamental relationship to beauty is, as Edwards everywhere insists, not primarily the enjoyment of it but the creation of it and participation in it. Central to the Edwardsean legacy, only recently beginning to find its heirs, is his pioneering exploration of that aesthetically articulated terrain. The dream of politics founded upon beauty is a recurrent one which may well be renewed among us by the very contrary qualities of our present experience. If so, we do well to take Jonathan Edwards as a companion and cartographer of the difficult passage from beauty to politics.

List of Abbreviations

Citations of works by Jonathan Edwards are given in the text of this essay, appearing between square brackets, using the following code, and referring to the pages in those editions. In the cases of the "Miscellanies" and the "Notes on the Mind" the citations refer to number rather than page. The same is true of citations of *Images* except for one instance in which it is indicated that the reference is to a page. The edition of *Works* to which reference is made below is *The Works of President Edwards,* a reprint of the Worcester edition of 1808–1809 with some additions, 4 vols. (New York, Leavitt & Allen, 1843).

Code	Title
EC	*Dissertation Concerning the End for Which God Created the World,* in *Works,* II, 191–257.
FJ	*Jonathan Edwards: Selections,* ed. by Clarence H. Faust and Thomas H. Johnson, rev. ed. (New York, Hill & Wang, 1962).
FW	*Freedom of the Will,* ed. by Paul Ramsey (New Haven, Yale University Press, 1957).
HA	*A Humble Attempt to Promote Explicit Agreement and Visible Union of God's People in Extraordinary Prayer,* in *Works,* III, 427–508.
Images	*Images or Shadows of Divine Things*, ed. by Perry Miller (New Haven, Yale University Press, 1948).
Mind	"Notes on the Mind," in Harvey G. Townsend (ed.), *The Philosophy of Jonathan Edwards From His Private Notebooks* (Eugene, University of Oregon Press, 1955).
Misc.	*Miscellanies,* Yale Collection of Edwards Manuscripts (Yale University Library).
OS	*The Great Christian Doctrine of Original Sin Defended,* in *Works,* II, 305–510.
RA	*Religious Affections,* ed. by John E. Smith (New Haven, Yale University Press, 1959).
TV	*The Nature of True Virtue,* ed. by William Frankena (Ann Arbor, University of Michigan Press, 1960).
WR	*A History of the Work of Redemption,* in *Works,* I, 293–516.

Individual, Civil Society, and State in American Transcendentalism

A. Robert Caponigri

The political and social thought of American transcendentalism retains a double motive of interest. The first motive is historical. Transcendentalism is an episode in the American story. It is an episode of many facets, not the least of which—and in some perspective the most important—is its character as an effort at a crucial moment of our country's development to understand the meaning and assess the character of the American experience. As such it possesses an abiding interest and importance for the American historical consciousness.

The second motive is speculative or theoretical. As a speculative effort, and in virtue of its basic speculative insights, transcendentalism raised anew a most ancient and persistent problem of western political thought. This is the problem of the intricate and dialectical relationships between the individual, the state, and the civil order or civil society. In virtue of its basic speculative insight—which we shall call the transcendentalist principle—transcendentalism effected a radical change in the classic western solution of this problem. Classically, the potentially explosive confrontation between individual and state—or morality and policy, as Thoreau phrases it,[1] conscience and coercive power—was mediated by the civil order, by civil society. At this point the transcendentalist and the classical views were to come into conflict.

Classically, the function of the civil order was mediatorial and constitutive. It comprised a wisdom, as Vico would have called it, or a jurisprudence, an order of civility, which established both state and individual—morality and policy—in the just autonomy of each and in the inter-relations which must prevail between them. It established the ambient in which the just claims and obligations as well as the dynamic interplay of these elements could be realized without violent impact or mutual confusion. This civil order was woven of a public philosophy reached by open dialogue, of consensus reached on the basis of this philosophy and stabilized in history, tradition, and authority. The concept of this order provided the proper and radical sense of the terms "civil" and "civility." "Civility" resided in the capacity to generate, sustain, and communicate such an order; the civil man, the *civis*, was the man formed and educated to partake in that order in all its aspects.

The radical result of the transcendentalist principle as it entered the world of men and of public action, of policy, to retain Thoreau's term, was the dissolution of the civil order conceived in this sense. It deprived public life of this mediatorial and constitutive principle. As a consequence, it left the other elements of this complex structure, individual and state, in stark confrontation without mediation. This result seriously affected the transcendentalist assessment of the American experience and of the actual condition and tasks of the American polity.

Transcendentalism, as might well be expected, was not unaware of the serious tension created by the dissolution of the civil order and the consequent unmediated confrontation of the elements of individual and state, of morality and policy, or coercive power. As a result, it found itself confronted by the further speculative task of redefining the kind of relations which should prevail between them or, in other words, of finding a principle, procedure, or structure which would fill the vacuum created by the dissolution of the civil order. This effort constitutes the constructive dimension and at the same time the inner speculative movement of transcendentalist political thought.

This is the movement we shall try to trace through its successive stages. The steps which must be taken in this task may be listed in the following manner: (a) the characterization of the transcendentalist principle, or of transcendentalism as principle; (b) the delineation of the process by which the transcendentalist principle entails the dissolution of the concept of the civil order, leaving the elements of individual and state, morality and policy, in unmediated confrontation; (c) the consequences which follow in the transcendentalist assessment of the American policy; (d) the identification of the attempts by transcendentalism to close the gap which has thus been opened by the transcendentalist principle. These, finally, prove to be the Thoreauvian doctrine of resistance to civil power as the means of moralizing policy; the Emersonian doctrine of the elite of character and the educative function of the state; and in conclusion, the Brownsonian rediscovery through the critique of the transcendentalist principle of the concept of civil order and the reassessment of the American political experience in terms of his theory of the constitution. We may begin by formulating in as brief and lapidary a manner as possible the transcendentalist principle.

No word occurs more frequently or is employed with greater emphasis in the idiom of transcendentalism than "principle." Nevertheless, no undertaking seems more resistant to happy results than that of stating the transcendentalist principle itself, although the innermost thrust of transcendentalism is to achieve the status of principle. This is especially true in the present context because the social and political implications of transcendentalism, both theoretical and critical, follow on transcendentalism not as "sentiment" or "enthusiasm," terms frequently employed to characterize it, but as principle. The formulation of this principle, consequently, the transcendentalist principle, though difficult, is imperative. Encouragement is lent by the view of its earliest historian, O. B. Frothingham. Qualifying Emerson's own view, Frothingham writes: "Transcendentalism was a distinct philosophical system. Practically it was an assertion of the inalienable worth of man; theoretically, it was an assertion of the immanence of divinity in instinct, the transfer of supernatural attributes to the natural constitution of mankind."[2]

Transcendentalism as principle concerns in essence man's access to truth. It asserts the direct revelation to the individual, in intuition, of truth of universal range and validity. This direct revelation or communication of truth may come to the individual by either, or both, of two ways. It may come by way of withdrawal to the inner sphere of consciousness (the position favored by Emerson).[3] It may also come by way of the immediate, indeed empathic and not unmystical, communion with physical nature, the Thoreauvian way.[4] These ways, of course, do not exclude each other.

One is assured of the intention of transcendentalism to advance itself as a philosophical principle by Emerson's effort to endow it with a respectable genealogy in the history of philosophy. He employs the distinction, which he asserts to be apodictic, between idealist and materialist to locate it dialectically. He appeals to the authority of Kant for its initial insights and to Jacobi, among others, for its rightness in the moral sphere. Frothingham endows it with an even ampler provenance.[5] The validity of these claims may be debated, especially Emerson's tendency to reduce the process of the critical philosophy of Kant to an assertion of the supremacy of "intuition." One feels that the "tough-minded" Kant, confronted with Emerson's views, would have been tempted to direct against them the heavy-handed satire he directed against Swedenborg.[6] Emerson, incidentally, assigns an extraordinarily elevated status in the history of thought to Swedenborg.[7] But this issue may be left to the historians to judge.[8]

Of greater importance to the character of transcendentalism as principle is the question of the seat and modes of communication of this intuition of universal truth. That seat is the individual, whether through interior illumination or through contemplation and communion with nature. This intuition, however, as Emerson explains, is not given the individual as a constant and constitutive element of consciousness. It is granted him, rather, in moments or flashes of interior illumination or insights into the processes of nature which are not his to command. These moments, when granted, lift the transcendentalist to heights of clear vision and wisdom; when they pass or are withheld, they leave him in that penumbral perplexity which Emerson poignantly describes.[9] The transcendentalist, by this account, dwells in a "chiaroscuro" of consciousness, exalted in moments of illumination but resting at other times in a faith that the "blue sky," in Emerson's words,[10] endures beyond the obscuring veils.

The intuitive revelation of truth possesses a purely formal character, for while, as Emerson notes,[11] it touches all that can transpire in experience, no dimension of experience, no content of experience, follows from it with necessity. The salient characteristic of this intuition is that it yields, not a personal and private and hence solipsistic truth, but a transcendental truth, in a sense reminiscent of, but not formally identifiable with, the Kantian meaning of that term as involving universality (that is, normativeness for all individual subjects), and necessity (that is, as involving in some way the inadmissibility of alternate

claims).[12] In the introspective or communicative moment
the individual is placed in the presence of, even in a kind
of possession of, the Fact, the unalterable and all-ground-
ing Fact, in Emerson's term.[13] This presence or possession
of transcendental truth (as transpiring *in* but not issuing
from the individual) lends to the vision and to the utterance (never perfect or even adequate) of the individual a
range and authority far outreaching his personal capacity;
indeed it makes these utterances normative for all men.
In that moment he becomes, as it were, the *medium* of
universal truth in a manner which again recalls Swedenborg and the shades of the wrath of Kant.

That everlasting and transcendent Fact is rendered
present to the individual through the contemplation of
nature, especially contemplation in solitude. Here it is the
testimony of Thoreau that is most weighty. Communion
with nature opens consciousness to the sense of the great
order which informs nature. By reason of this continuity
with nature—his indwelling in nature and nature's indwelling in him—indeed its rising to self-consciousness
in him, nature ought to find its fullest realization in the
human subject. Nature performs all her works, works all
her miracles, produces all her effects by the silent outflow
of her power from the secret source which is her essence
without reliance on aught but herself. Nature works tran-
quilly and silently; she multiplies her wonders before our
eyes with a flow of spontaneous energy which is neither
clamorous nor ostentatious. This secret power and silent
creative process of nature is also the secret power and the
silent inward creative process of the transcendentalist.
The rhythm and silent flow of effortless creative energy
revealed in nature is the very pattern upon which he
would shape his own life. More precisely, perhaps, the vo-
cation of the transcendentalist is to permit the creative
energy of nature to release itself in him. He, too, is nature.

He is perhaps nature's highest moment—the moment in which the silent outflow of creative energy reaches its culmination, becoming a conscious, a self-conscious, and not merely a physical or animate law.

What is the effect upon the transcendentalist? With what qualities or properties, what potentialities, does this release of the power and the order of nature endow him? These are, saliently, self-reliance and character—two intimately related, but not identifiable, concepts.

The whole ethics of transcendentalism, Emerson writes, is to be self-dependent, on the model of nature.[14] This self-dependence does not, however, immure the individual in a solipsistic isolation. Rather, it arouses an echo of the Kantian categorical imperative: "To believe your own thought, to believe that what is true for you in your private heart is true for all men—that is genius."[15] This self-reliance is not a form of egotism. The transcendentalist is self-dependent precisely because he is not an egotist. He is self-reliant because he humbly recognizes the universal truth which speaks in him and through him, of which he is the bearer but not the source. The self becomes more truly self, the more it recognizes itself as the seat of the epiphany of this universal truth which both annuls and establishes the self—annuls it egotistically to establish it transcendentally.

This self in its transcendentality is not, in turn, given to man as a sure endowment, an abiding gift, a substantial identity. It is countered by a tendency to fly the true universal which speaks in the secret heart and in the miracles of nature, to hearken to the clamorous voice from without, to the babble of opinion—the false universal of Hegel in one of its aspects.[16] Character, the second pillar of transcendentalist ethics, springs from this dialectic: the tension and distention of the self between inner and outer, between society and solitude. Man achieves character to the degree to which he achieves reliance upon the inner light, the inner voice, and resists temptation to seek truth outside himself, in the clamor of the multivoiced world of opinion. To the degree to which he achieves character, he becomes the lawgiver to himself, not subservient to any outer law.[17]

The crucial test of this view of man and of his access to truth, of the transcendentalist principle, arises at the point at which the self-reliant man leave his solitude and enters the world of civility, of public truth and action. The most sweeping consequence of this encounter is the ideal dissolution, that is, the dissolution in its idea, of the civil order, or civil society.

Interestingly enough, this consequence is contrary to a first expectation aroused by the transcendentalist principle. The natural expectation is that universal truth, speaking in the private heart (in Emerson's phrase) of each man on issuing into the world of men would find a universal echo and generate that domain of public truth which constitutes the elemental structure of the civil order. Thus a civil world would eventuate, a world of civility, of consensus, founded on the fact that each man, speaking his own, utters also the universal truth. Within the framework of this discourse the institutions of civility, which mediate all claims and obligations and dialectically relate morality and policy, individual and state, would arise. Emerson hints as much in his short verse: "Character":

> He spoke, and words more soft than rain,
> Brought the Age of Gold again,[18]

that golden age which forms one of the most enduring and cherished myths of mankind.

This expectation, however, is frustrated. Carried to its conclusion, the transcendentalist principle effects rather the ideal dissolution of the concept of the civil order, making of that golden age a delusion rather than a myth. Our concern now is with the steps by which this dissolution is effected. These steps involve one by one the processes by which the civil order is constituted and sustained; these are: the public philosophy, history, tradition, and authority. To comprehend more clearly this process of dissolution, it may be worthwhile, before taking up these steps in turn, to delineate more precisely, but briefly, the notion of the civil order, of civility, and its function.

The notion of the civil order rests on the perception of that distinction between morality and policy which Thoreau recognizes. It rests further on the perception that these two factors have a very particular characteristic: they cannot be resolved without residue the one into the other, nor can they exist and function in sheer confrontation or juxtaposition. The reason lies in the fact that they both, morality and policy, come to focus in a single point, human action, alike individual and group, and both establish claims upon and generate obligation, erecting normative principles for such action. Finally, the civil order rests upon the reality of the public sphere, in which the consequences of morality and policy meet and intermingle.

The consequence of this characteristic is that morality and policy must be mediated. The civil order is precisely that order in which such mediation between morality and policy, between individual and state is effected, and effected in such wise that the native autonomy of each and the intricate interplay of both is established. Civility is that condition, or quality, of human association in which such mediation is effected and prevails. Civil wisdom, or prudence, is the process of establishing the principles, norms, and procedures of such mediation between morality and policy and of translating these into the complex institutions of civil society.

It is to be noted that the civil order, while it generates the order of institutions, is not to be identified without residue with any particular set of institutions. It is transcendent to all such sets and is the norm by which they are judged in their various qualities. The civil order is essentially an order of principles, the specific force of which is to generate the highly dialectical unity between thought and action under diverse conditions of time and of necessity in such wise that the quality of civility endures through changes. The fact that the civil order is essentially an order of principles does not, however, preclude the quest for the common or normative institutions of civility. This is a quest which has always beguiled philosophers and while the prey is elusive, the quest goes on. The ideal state of Plato, the religion, solemn marriage, and the burial of the dead in the genial insights of Vico, and the many other such insights which history records, are legitimate terms of this quest, though the claims of any one cannot be allowed as absolute.

By reason of its character as a mediatorial process, the notion of the civil order involves certain presuppositions as the basis of its actualization, exhibits certain properties which cannot be destroyed without involving the destruction of that order itself and hence returning morality and policy to that unmediated state in which they confront each other as hostile and mutually exclusive elements. The first of these conditions is the public character of truth and the capacity of establishing a public philosophy on the public character of truth. The second is that the social processes in which this public philosophy is realized exhibit a time-ideal dimension, that is, that the ideality and normative force of the principles of civility emerge in human consciousness and inform human action in an historical process in which the ideal principles and the demands of concrete action are temporarily mediated.

History and civility, as Vico has demonstrated, are indissolubly linked. The third condition is tradition. Tradition is the dimension of civility in which the principles established in the time-ideal order of history are given effective continuity and are communicated. Tradition is essentially an economic process; that is, it reduces the mediatorial principles of the civil order to forms in which they can be communicated and perpetuated without a re-enactment of the process by which those principles were formed. Finally, the civil order is marked by the character of authority. Authority is not an unmediated act of will, but an act mediated by the public philosophy.

The transcendentalist principle effects the ideal dissolution of the civil order because its theory of man's access to truth through private revelation (the term is Emerson's own: "We distinguish the announcements of the soul, its manifestations of its own nature, by the term Revelation"; again, "Revelation is the disclosure of the soul"[19] more or less directly undermines each of these elements of the civil order in turn.

In the first place the transcendentalist principle inhibits the formation of a truly public philosophy. Emerson speaks of the encounter of private insight with private insight and their coincidence:

. . . tomorrow a stranger will say with masterly good sense precisely what we have thought and felt all the time and we shall be forced to take with shame our own opinion from another.[20]

Such coincidence, however, is merely occasionalistic. It does not constitute a public truth because it exhibits no law or principle by which this coincidence is regulated and assured. A public philosophy, such as the civil order requires, demands just such a principle and all the great civil philosophers have directed their enquiries toward the discovery of that principle.

In similar fashion the historical basis of civil order is undermined. No better example of this process can be found, perhaps, than Emerson's own essay on history. While opening the essay with the sage remark that "man is explicable by nothing less than all his history,"[21] as the exposition proceeds, this position is entirely reversed. It proves to be that man, the individual man, in the light of his inner revelation, deciphers history: "Civil and natural history . . . must be explained from individual history or remain mere words. . . ."[22]

The individual gives meaning and reality to history by discovering in it the confirmation of what is original in himself. History is thus transformed from time-ideal process to symbolic enactment of the universal mind present wholly in the individual. From history the individual draws comfort and illumination, but no original truth. The essence of the civil order, however, is the capacity of the time-ideal process of history to generate a normative and mediating truth which is not antecedently accessible to the individual.

The transcendentalist principle, in like manner, transforms tradition from a living mediating force into an incubus upon the individual which alienates him from himself, blinding him to the inner light and burdening him with a dead wisdom which he cannot inform with new life. It forces him to imitate himself and not to live in that eternal present which is the native milieu of the transcendentalist.[23]

This process of the annulment of the elements of the civil order culminates in the rejection of authority. Authority, in the light of the transcendentalist principle, becomes the royal questioner of Diogenes; it stands between him and his sun, the inner light. It is the complete annihilation of his self-dependency, for in the view of the transcendentalist principle authority is the complete other, with which there can be no compromise or conciliation. Authority is the ideally unmediated will of the other and carries with it no warranty from the universal mind. It comes close to being that practical lie of which Emerson speaks, and which has its paradigm in the dogma of Plato's *Republic*.[24]

If this is the process by which the civil order is dissolved in its idea by the transcendentalist principle, what are the consequences of this dissolution? The principal consequences are two: the first is the reduction of the principle of the state as the agent of policy to expediency; the second is the reduction of morality and polity to that original condition of unmediated confrontation and alienation which the civil order was meant to heal.

"Government is at best but an expedient," Thoreau says in the lecture "Resistance to Civil Government."[25] This sentiment becomes the leitmotiv, not only of this, but of all his essays and lectures germane to the question. The state, the institutional agency of government or public policy, does nothing of its own initiative; rather it is an impediment to the initiative of individuals and groups acting on their own.[26] The state is not for all that without a principle of necessity, but this necessity is only the need of the people for some complicated machinery to satisfy their idea of government.[27] The state, despite this necessity, has no ideal principle proper to itself; when its true character is revealed, as in the idea or the practice of majority rule, its only principle proves to be superior force.[28] At best government and the state are an expedient by which men would fain succeed in leaving each other alone; and when government is most expedient, the governed are most let alone by it.[29]

Emerson is no less, but perhaps even more, emphatic in his affirmation of this same idea. For him it is unintelligent brute force which lies at the basis of society.[30] Society everywhere is in conspiracy against the manhood of every one of its members.[31] Man to be a man must be a nonconformist; no law can be sacred save that which he legislates to himself. The civilized man has built a coach and lost the use of his legs; society is good when it does not violate me, best when it is most like solitude; he who has the Lawgiver (the inner light) may with safety not only neglect, but even contravene, every written commandment; the transcendentalist shuns society and finds his tasks and his amusements in solitude: he is not a good citizen, and Emerson is completely at one with Thoreau in the resounding assertion that the less government the better and that that government is best which governs not at all.[32]

Expressions such as these, reiterating in various ways the single idea of government and of the state as mere expediency, could be multiplied. It is more important, however, to examine the basis and import of this assertion than to review such expressions. What is the essential meaning of expediency in this context and in what sense does it properly define the principle of the state? The reply to this query cannot be drawn from the general language of political thought but must be sought within the proper idiom of transcendentalism.

Expedience in that idiom means an order of thought and action unilluminated by the inner light and hence containing no ideal principle, no gleam of the universal truth. It is thought and action ordered to mere contingency and utility. The opposite of the expedient is the moral, which is the will illuminated by the universal mind. As the state is the organ of expediency, conscience is the organ of moral insight and will. The expedient possesses no ideality in itself; it arises, rather, in those moments of the obscuring of the inner light which we have noted in Emerson's exposition of the transcendentalist principle. When that inner illumination is enkindled anew, the essential unreality of the expedient becomes apparent. In this sense, proper to transcendentalism, the notion of expediency is applicable to the state in two ways. The state is mere expediency in its origin and it is mere expediency in the range of the claims it can make, the obligation it can engender.

Expediency lies at the basis of the state, is its origin, because the realm of morality, of illumination by the inner light of universal mind, contains intrinsic limits. That illumination is given to man, as we have seen, not as a constant and constitutive element of his being, but intermittently in those "gleams of the light within" for which, as Emerson writes, man must watch and which he must learn to detect. It is in the moments of obscurity, induced by the intermittency of this inward illumination, that the expedient appears. Expedience is, therefore, essentially a negative or limiting concept in the transcendentalist context; it is not ideality but the absence of ideality. In these moments of obscurity, of the absence of inner illumination, the expedient appears in two forms, as force and as utility. These, rather than conscience and morality, become in those moments the motive principles of human action, and the state (government) policy is but the institutionalized form of this activity.

For this reason, as Emerson writes,[33] the state is by its nature meant to disappear, as wisdom in the person of the wise man broadens the range of illumination and extends the sway of universal truth, though this disappearance, as Thoreau notes, is a horizon concept, since man has no power to evoke that inner revelation of universal mind. As a consequence the authority of the state is an "impure" one, not a moral authority transcendentally grounded.[34] Policy is the organized form of public action on the ground of expedience, of force and utility, in the absence of the illumination of conscience. The state is the organ of policy.

In view of its basis in expediency in this sense Thoreau's notion of the necessity of the state, noted earlier, must be revised. Expedience, the state and government, policy have a deeper necessity than he there assigns them, precisely because of those intrinsic limitations of the inner light. Policy has its necessity in the very dialectic of transcendentality.

The state is mere expediency also in the range of claim it can advance, in the range and quality of the obligation it can engender. Thoreau quotes Paley on this point,[35] though with qualified approval. The state can make no claims upon the individual save those which fall within the range of expediency, which are matters of pure policy, that is, where action is dictated by utility or force and not by the guidance of conscience. Beyond the realm of expedience and the power of the state lies the vast realm of justice, and Thoreau accuses Paley of limiting his vision to that of expedience alone. He is at one with Paley, however, that in this range of expedience the claims of the state are valid. His point ultimately will be that in matters of justice the state cannot prevail; a higher obligation appears which may take the phenomenal form of resistance to the state—a notion which must be clarified.

These reflections lead us to the second consequence of the definition of the state as mere expedience. The situation of direct, unmediated confrontation, between morality and policy is reintroduced. The essential point is that each of these, morality and policy, contains a principle or ground of necessity, and both come to focus at the point of human action. Their direct, unmediated confrontation constitutes the essential ambiguity, the inner tension, of the human situation in the transcendentalist context, because the transcendentalist principle establishes no process of mediation between them. It is Manichean in this aspect, dividing human action into two realms of light and darkness which are essentially at war.

The transcendentalists were most sensitive to the condition of American society. Their animadversions upon it touch the most sensitive points: slavery, the problem of states rights, the emergence of class tensions, and others. It would be an undertaking of considerable interest to review and evaluate these animadversions in detail. Of greater importance for our theme, however, is to try to reach the root criticism and to determine in its light the penetration of transcendentalist criticism into the actual condition and needs of American society.

All of its single criticisms of American society and its political system, which culminate in the extreme statement of Thoreau that a man cannot without disgrace be associated with it,[36] add up to a single censure, which is never stated by the transcendentalist in explicit terms: American society, the American political system, provides no principle for the mediation of morality and policy, conscience and expedience; that is to say, it is unsustained by a civil order. As a consequence, the transcendentalists' assessment of the American system appears astigmatic. Its vision does not come to focus on the true situation of American society, namely, that such a civil order was its basic need, its absence the source of all the flaws they detected in it, and that its internal struggles could be justly evaluated only as efforts to generate such an order. This astigmatism was no accident; it was induced by the transcendentalist principle.

To this point it is the *pars destruens* of the transcendentalist approach to society and politics which has been emphasized: namely, the dissolution of the concept of the civil order, the reduction of the state to expediency (in the transcendentalist sense defined above), the indiscernment of the true situation and basic need of American society. But this *pars destruens* does not exhaust the transcendentalist effort. It too has its *pars construens* in the light of which alone its character can be fully delineated.

The starting point of the *pars construens* of transcendentalism is its recognition that, while morality and policy are, as Thoreau affirms, different and distinct, they cannot be left in that state of hostile confrontation in which the transcendentalist principle has placed them. The mediation of morality and policy, of conscience and expediency, individual and state, is a speculative imperative which transcendentalism accepts. The effort to meet this imperative constitutes the *pars construens* of transcendentalist thought. The fruit of these efforts can be traced in three conceptions of that principle of mediation: the notion of resistance to civil government in Thoreau, the elitism of character, or the wise man, of Emerson, and, finally, in the rediscovery of the civil order by Brownson and his effort in *The American Republic* to make it the interpretative key to the true structure and dynamics of the American constitution.

A serious editorial error was committed when the title of Thoreau's celebrated lecture was altered from "Resistance to Civil Government" to "Civil Disobedience." This alteration obscures the force and intent of Thoreau's thought. It slants that intent in a negative direction, toward an ultimate anarchism. The true thrust of Thoreau's thought is positive. It lies in the direction of the discovery of a principle of mediation between morality and policy not toward anarchy. In Thoreau's own words he demands "not at once no government, but *at once* a better government."[37]

The clue to the positive element in Thoreau's position, we believe, is to be found in two passages of the lecture "Resistance to Civil Government." The first is the qualification which he places on Paley's view on civil obligation. The second is the visionary passage with which the same lecture closes. In the first passage he notes: "Paley never appears to have contemplated those cases in which the rule of expediency does not apply, in which a people, as well as an individual, must do justice, come what may."[38] In the second he writes, "I please myself with imagining a state at last which can afford to be just to all men. . . ."[39] Somewhere between these two points the positive emphasis of the notion of resistance to civil government, that is, its character as a principle of mediation between morality and policy, falls.

To seize this point it is necessary to recur to the transcendentalist principle itself: that the individual is the repository of the revelation of universal mind and its truth and that the source of the expediency of the state lies in the limits inherent in this revelation. The positive duty of the individual is to make justice prevail over expediency, as the example of the drowning men illustrates.[40] But what channels are open to him to this end? One is the path of reform on which Thoreau looks with jaundiced eye.[41] The other is the path of resistance, which may take either a passive or an assertive form. While Thoreau himself is little inclined to the latter in any extreme form, his impassioned apology for John Brown is proof that for him even violence can be a justifiable form of resistance.[42]

Resistance, however, is but a phenomenal form. It is the form in which, under the given condition that the higher truth is revealed to the individual, that truth can be made to appear as the transcendental limit to the expediency of the state. But the noumenal principle of resistance is the extension of that universal truth. The positive function of resistance is not to pose a limit to the state as expedience, but to release the power of truth into the realm of policy. Gandhi, whose debt to Thoreau has often been remarked and explicitly acknowledged by himself, interpreted resistance in this fashion. He recognized the phenomenal form of resistance, seeing behind it and informing it, a positive principle, his own notion of "Satyagraha," the "force of truth."[43] Resistance to civil government is the channel for the release of this force of truth into the world of policy. It brings the moral conscience to bear upon the calculations of expediency and extends the realm of universal mind and its truth beyond the limits inherent in the basic mode of its revelation to the individual. Actually, resistance is positive, for it opposes force to force, the force of truth to that brute force in which, as Emerson says, the ultimate basis of the state is to be found. Conscience and expediency, morality and policy, individual and state are thus mediated, though the form of mediation is tense and falls short of synthesis.

The negative attitude of Emerson toward the state, harsh as it at times appears, is, nevertheless, only the obverse side of his integral position. The positive aspect of his thought is an effort to establish a principle of mediation between morality and policy. This principle takes the form of his concept of the elitism of character and of the myth of the wise man. The state will take on moral stature and become a moral force from a merely brute force, its enactments will reflect the illumination of universal truth rather than the dictates of mere expediency, when character prevails in public life, when the wise man and the man of policy are one. The passage in which this conception is expounded deserves to be quoted directly, for no paraphrase can achieve the suavity of Emerson's own expression:

Hence the less government we have the better—the fewer laws and the less confided power. The antidote to this abuse of formal government is the influence of private character, the growth of the individual; the appearance of the principle to supersede the proxy; the appearance of the wise man, of whom the existing government is, it must be owned, but a shabby imitation. That which all things tend to educe; which freedom, cultivation, intercourse, revolutions, go to form and deliver is character; that is the end of Nature, to reach unto this coronation of her king. To educate the wise man the State exists, and with the appearance of the wise man the State expires. The appearance of character makes the State unnecessary. The wise man is the State. . . . The power of love, as the basis of a state, has never been tried. . . . According to the order of nature . . . it stands thus; there will always be a government of force where men are selfish; and when they are pure enough to abjure the code of force they will be wise enough to see how . . . public ends . . . can be answered. . . . There is not, among the most religious and instructed men of the most religious and civil nations, a reliance on the moral sentiment and a sufficient belief in the unity of things, to persuade them that society can be maintained without artificial restraints as well as the solar system. . . .[44]

This is his version of the reign of the philosopher-king. In a sense this vision goes beyond mediation, or more accurately perhaps, reaches the state of pure mediation in the reign of love.

The flaw in this vision is apparent and not unlike the flaw which mars its remote prototype: the reign of the philosopher-king in Plato. This flaw is a circularity which negates the power of the original assertion. Emerson holds that the total mediation of morality and policy would flow from the presence and sway of the wise man, and the state would be thus redeemed from its condition of expediency, not in the half-hearted manner of the reformers (all of whom admit in some manner the supremacy of the bad state[45]) but completely. At the same time he holds that "to educate the wise man the State exists, and with the appearance of the wise man the State expires"[46]. The state must educate the wise man and in that very process prepare its own demise and dissolution. This circularity is paradoxical. Whence would the state, at whose basis lies brute power and whose whole principle is expediency, draw the resources to educate the wise man? Does not the notion of the self-dissolution of the state violate the deeper law of power (to which theorists of politics almost unanimously attest), namely, that power tends not only to preserve itself but to extend its sway? The presence of the wise man is the precondition of the state's transformation from force and expediency; yet the state itself has the mission of forming the wise man. The remedy of this paradoxical circularity is nowhere to be found in Emerson. The positive thrust of his thought, nevertheless, appears here: It is to find a principle by which the stark confrontation of morality and policy, of conscience and expediency, of state and individual, is mediated.

The strength of a philosophical system is evidenced nowhere so clearly as in its capacity for self-criticism. By this standard transcendentalism must be recognized as a strong system, for in the thought of Orestes Brownson it exhibits this capacity in a marked degree. From within transcendentalism itself Brownson initiates a process of criticism of its principle, which leads eventually to a recovery of the concept of the civil order as the mediating principle of morality and policy, of the relation between citizen and state. This recovery is effected through the re-establishment of those principles, public truth, history, tradition, and authority, upon which civil society rests. In another context the effort has been made to retrace the stages through which these principles are re-established by Brownson.[47] In the present context, it would seem more relevant to indicate briefly the way in which Brownson invokes the notion of the civil order, of civil society, in his theory of the American polity and its consitution, because in this theory all of those principles are seen at work.

The crux of Brownson's theory of the American constitution lies in his distinction between the written and the "unwritten" constitution.[48] It is a fallacy, to which the founding fathers of the Republic, in Brownson's view, had fallen victim, to imagine that the Republic rests upon the written constitution, that it has been called into being by an act of convention or contract. The act of convention, from which the written constitution eventuates is preceded by a process far more profound, the establishment of the American people or *civil society*.[49]

This people, or *civil society*, is to be distinguished both from the government and from the abstract individual, whose notion underlay the theory of the origin of the nation by convention. Government is rather the ordination of civil society.[50] The formation of civil society is a long and complex historical process. Only the historical identity thus established empowers the sovereign people, civil society, to establish in turn the constitution of government and the status of the individual as citizen. This civil society establishes both state and citizen in their respective autonomy and in their relationships vis-à-vis each other and mediates the interplay of claim and obligation between them. The function of civil society is to secure at once the authority of the public order and the freedom of the individual citizen, the sovereignty of the people without social despotism and individual freedom without anarchy.[51] Its function is to bring into dialectical union authority and liberty, the natural rights of man and the rights of society.[52]

A constitution in which this ideal has been realized has not, before the American experience, appeared in history. Ancient republics asserted the state to the detriment of the individual; modern republics either repeat this error or assert the individual to the detriment of the state. It is the particular mission, providentially ordained, of the American republic to actualize this ideal, to realize in its polity the freedom of each, individual and state, with advantage to the other.[53]

This unique character and mission of the United States has been overlooked and misunderstood by the great majority even of our own statesmen.[54] Indeed, the very men who composed the written constitution exhibit this lack of understanding. They misprised the character of their own action; as a consequence, the theoretical concepts by which they sought to explain and justify that action and define its consequences cannot be taken as clues to the interpretation of the constitution.[55] This miscomprehension can be traced to no other source than a failure to understand the notion of civil society, the historical process which gives rise to it, and the exclusive capacity with which it is endowed to establish both government and citizen. Through this civil order alone can their respective claims and the respective claims of morality and policy be mediated, for it is the civil order which establishes each and defines their respective spheres.

A dual weakness, consequently, seems to afflict the political and social thought of transcendentalism as represented by Thoreau and Emerson. The first is a deficiency at the level of theory, the second, at the level of the concrete analysis and evaluation of the American experience. These deficiencies are closely related.

At the level of theory, the elaboration of the basic principle of transcendentalism—its theory of man's access to truth—leads to serious imbalance and internal divorcement among the elements: citizen, civil society, and state. Individual and state are brought into sharp confrontation because of the absence of a valid principle of mediation. This line of thought leads in turn to the concept of the state as pure expediency, harboring no ideal principle in itself. Classically, this principle of mediation is the civil order, civil society. The transcendentalist theory of Thoreau and Emerson leaves the concept of the civil order undeveloped; it is forced to excogitate alternate principles of mediation on whatever basis the transcendentalist principle could provide.

This theoretical deficiency or limitation accounts for the corresponding limitation at the level of the concrete assessment and characterization of the American polity. A more nearly adequate conception of the civil order would have indicated to Thoreau and Emerson at what point the actual weakness of American polity lay; namely, that it had not, after its revolutionary origins (which, in the last analysis, could only be justified on the basis of a sound notion of the civil order) adequately comprehended its civil origins and that the real task before it was to redefine its own character on the basis of that order. Only thus could it truly understand the perplexing and harassing problems which bedeviled it, specifically those of slavery and states rights.

The political and social thought of Brownson, specifically his theory of the American polity, suggests itself as an effort, with its roots in transcendentalism itself, to correct both these deficiencies. Brownson, through his critique of the transcendentalist principle, rediscovered the concept of the civil order with its constitutive and mediating functions. On this basis he was able to offer an assessment of the American experience and a theory of the American polity in which the sharp unmediated confrontations of transcendentalist theory were transcended and the speciously conflicting claims of state and individual, conscience and policy, reconciled.

Footnotes

1. "Will mankind never learn that policy is not morality?" in "Slavery in Massachusetts" in *The Writings of Henry David Thoreau: Reform*

Papers, ed. by Wendell Glick (Princeton, Princeton University Press, 1973), 104 (hereafter cited as *Reform Papers*).

2. *Transcendentalism in New England* (New York, Harper and Row, 1959), 136.

3. "His thought—*that* is the universe. His experience inclines him to behold the procession of facts you call the world as flowing perpetually outward from an invisible, unsounded centre in himself, centre alike of him and of them, and necessitating him to regard all things as having a subjective or relative existence, relative to that aforesaid Unknown Centre of him" ("The Transcendentalist" in *Essays and Poems*, ed. by G. F. Maine [London, Collins, 1965], 299) (hereafter cited as *Essays and Poems*).

4. Cf. Norman Foerster, *Nature in American Literature* (New York, Macmillan, 1923) 101. "Thus it was not to study the fauna and flora of Middlesex County that Thoreau spent his life. . . . What . . . brought him out in all weathers . . . was the mystic's hope of detecting 'some trace of the Ineffable'" (p. 102). . . . This Izaak Walton of the soul."

5. Cf. *Essays and Poems*, "The Transcendentalist," 301–302 for Kant; 300 for Jacobi; and Frothingham, *Transcendentalism*, chapters I–V inclusive.

6. Cf. Immanuel Kant, *Dreams of a Ghost-seer Explained by the Dreams of a Metaphysician* (1766).

7. "The moral insight of Swedenborg, the correction of popular errors, the announcement of ethical laws take him out of comparison with any other modern writer, and entitle him to a place, vacant for some ages, among the lawgivers of mankind," in *Representative Men*: "Swedenborg: The Mystic" (in *Essays and Poems*, 364).

8. Cf. Lewis White Beck, *Early German Philosophy: Kant and His Predecessors* (Cambridge, Harvard University Press, Belknap Press, 1969), *passim* but especially Part II, Chapter VIII and Part III, Chapter XVII.

9. Cf. *Essays and Poems*, "The Transcendentalist," 307.

10. "What am I? What but a thought of serenity and independence, an abode in the deep blue sky? Presently, the clouds shut down again; yet we retain the belief that this pretty web we weave will at last be overshot and reticulated with veins of blue. . . . Patience . . . is for us. . . . Patience, and still patience" (*Essays and Poems*, "The Transcendentalist," 307–308).

11. *Essays and Poems*.

12. For the Kantian sense of transcendentality, cf. L. W. Beck, *Early German Philosophy*, 409–37 *passim*, especially 413–14.

13. ". . . I feel like other men my relation to that Fact which cannot be spoken or defined, or even thought, but which exists and will exist" (*Essays and Poems*, "The Transcendentalist," 299).

14. "From this transfer of the world into consciousness, this beholding

all things in the mind, follows easily his whole ethics. It is simply to be self-dependent (*ibid.*, "The Transcendentalist," 299).

15. *Ibid.*, "Self-Reliance," 38.

16. "I was at my old tricks, the selfish member of a selfish society. . . . I wish to exchange this flash-of-lightning faith for continuous daylight, this fever glow for a benign climate" (*ibid.*, "The Transcendentalist," 307). For the "false universal" in Hegel cf. J. N. Findlay, *The Philosophy of Hegel* (New York, Collier Books, 1966), 227–30.

17. "No law can be sacred to me but that of my nature" (*Essays and Poems*, "Self-Reliance," 40).

18. *Ibid.*, "Character," 501.

19. *Ibid.*, "The Oversoul," 136–37.

20. *Ibid.*, "Self-Reliance," 38.

21. *Ibid.*, "History," 21.

22. *Ibid.*, "History," 27.

23. "What have I to do with the sacredness of tradition, if I live wholly from within?" (*ibid.*, "Self-Reliance,' 40).

24. Cf. *Ibid.*, 262.

25. *Reform Papers*, "Resistance to Civil Government," 63.

26. "This government never of itself furthered any enterprise, but by the alacrity with which it got out of its way" (*ibid.*, "Resistance to Civil Government," 64).

27. "But it is not the less necessary for this; for the people must have some complicated machinery or other, and hear its din." (*ibid.*, "Resistance to Civil Government," 63–64).

28. "After all . . . when . . . a majority are permitted . . . to rule, [it] is not because they are most likely to be in the right . . . but because they are physically the strongest" (*ibid.*, "Resistance to Civil Government," 64).

29. *Ibid.* "Resistance to Civil Government," 64. The Paley quoted on page 67 by Thoreau is William Paley (1743–1805), British theologian and moralist (*Principles of Moral and Political Philosophy*, 1785).

30. *Essays and Poems*, "Self-Reliance," 43.

31. *Ibid.*, "Self-Reliance," 40.

32. Cf. for Emerson, *Essays and Poems*, 40, 55, 299, 300, 302, 305, 366; for Thoreau, *Reform Papers*, 63.

33. Cf. *Essays and Poems*, 263.

34. Cf. *Reform Papers*, 89.

35. Cf. *ibid.*, "Resistance to Civil Government," 67–68.

36. "How does it become a man to behave toward this American government today? I answer that he cannot without disgrace be associated with it" (*ibid.*, "Resistance to Civil Government," 67.

37. "But to speak practically and as a citizen, unlike those who call themselves no-government men, I ask for, not at once no government, but *at once* a better government" (*ibid.*, 64).

38. Cf. *ibid.*, 68.

39. Cf. *ibid.*, 90.

40. Cf. *ibid.*, 68.

41. Cf. *Reform Papers,* "Reform and Reformers" 181–97; "The Reformer, the impersonation of disorder and imperfection" (p. 182); "The modern Reformers are a class of *improvvisánti* more wonderful and amusing than the Italians" (p. 185).

42. Cf. *ibid.*, 111ff., especially page 124.

43. For Gandhi cf. B. R. Nanda, *Mahatma Gandhi: A Biography* (Boston, Beacon Press, 1958); Horace Alexander, *Gandhi through Western Eyes* (New York, Asia Pub. House, 1969); E. H. Erikson, *Gandhi's Truth: On the Origins of Militant Non-violence* (New York, Norton, 1969).

44. Cf. *Essays and Poems*, 263, 264.

45. Cf. *ibid.*, 265.

46. Cf. *ibid.*, 263.

47. Cf. A. R. Caponigri, "Brownson and Emerson: Nature and History" in *American Transcendentalism*, ed. by Brian M. Barbour (Notre Dame, University of Notre Dame Press, 1973); Thomas I. Cooke and Arnaud B. Leavelle, "Orestes A. Brownson's *The American Republic*" in *The Review of Politics*, Vol. IV (1942), 77–90 and 173–93.

48. "The constitution of the United States is twofold: written and unwritten, the constitution of the people and the constitution of the government," in Orestes A. Brownson, *The American Republic*, ed. by Americo D. Lapati (New Haven, College and University Press, 1972), 143 (hereafter cited as ARLIpati).

49. "The constitution of the people as one people . . . precedes the convention and it is the unwritten constitution, the providential constitution of the American people or civil society, as distinguished from the constitution of the government, which . . . is the ordination of civil society. . . . The unwritten constitution is the creation or constitution of the sovereign (people) . . . which constitutes in turn, the government . . . which is clothed with just so much . . . authority as the sovereign . . . ordains" (*ibid.*, 156).

50. Cf. *ibid.*

51. "Secures . . . the true idea of the state which secures at once the authority of the public and the freedom of the individual—the sovereignty of the people without social despotism and individual freedom without anarchy" (ARLIpati, 33).

52. *Ibid.*

53. "The Greek and Roman Republics asserted the state to the detriment of individual freedom; modern republics either do the same or assert individual freedom to the detriment of the state. The American republic has been instituted by Providence to realize the freedom of each with advantage to the other" (*ibid.*).

54. *Ibid.*

55. "But the philosophy, the theory of government, the understanding of the framers of the constitution, must be considered. . . . *obiter dicta.* . . . Their political philosophy, their political theory . . . forms no rule for interpreting their work. Their work was inspired by and accords with the historical fact and is authorized and explained by them" (ARLIpati, 155). (One recalls the *"ipsis rebus dictantibus"* of Tacitus and Vico and the *"come stanno le cose"* of Machiavelli.)

American Pragmatism Before and After 1898

Max H. Fisch

I.

Prologue

In this country, at least, it was in 1898 that the word "pragmatism" was first used in a public address and then in print as the name of a philosophic doctrine and method. The history of American pragmatism was thereby divided into two quite different periods: a period without the name pragmatism or any other public name, from about 1865 to 1898, and a period with that name and several others, from 1898 onward. Among the other names are practicalism, pragmaticism, absolute pragmatism, humanism, voluntarism, functionalism, contextualism, instrumentalism, experimentalism, operationalism.

The differences between the two periods are very great. In the second period pragmatism became a movement, the liveliest movement so far in American philosophy. That was due in large part, no doubt, to its having evangelists like James and schools like Dewey's at the University of Chicago. But it was due in no small part to its having a name, which served both as a flag for its followers and as a target for its critics.

The epoch-marking address was by William James. It was the annual address before the Philosophical Union at the University of California in Berkeley on August 26, 1898. It was published in September. The title was "Philosophical Conceptions and Practical Results."[1] The members of the Union were, as usual, prepared by having devoted the preceding academic year to critical study of the speaker's philosophy, as represented in this case by James's *The Will to Believe and Other Essays in Popular Philosophy*, fresh from the press in 1897, dedicated to his "old friend" Charles Sanders Peirce. At the last meeting of the year, in May, the president of the Union, George H. Howison, had presented his own criticisms of the title essay.

Let us imagine ourselves as members of the Philosophical Union, thus prepared, attending James's address, reading it soon afterwards, being moved by it, working backward through the first period to its origins, and living forward into the second period.

II.

James's Address

The lecture hall is Harmon Gymnasium. There are over a thousand persons present. James is introduced by President Howison. After some opening remarks on philosophers as pathfinders and trail blazers, James is saying to us:

I will seek to define with you merely what seems to be the most likely direction in which to start upon the trail of truth. Years ago this direction was given to me by an American philosopher whose home is in the East, and whose published works, few as they are and scattered in periodicals, are no fit expression of his powers. I refer to Mr. Charles S. Peirce, with whose very existence as a philosopher I dare say many of you are unacquainted. He is one of the most original of contemporary thinkers; and the principle of practicalism—or pragmatism, as he called it, when I first heard him enunciate it at Cambridge in the early '70's—is the clue or compass by following which I find myself more and more confirmed in believing we may keep our feet upon the proper trail.

James then presents "Peirce's principle" as he says Peirce himself introduced it in the *Popular Science*

Monthly for January 1878. James then says: "This is the principle of Peirce, the principle of pragmatism. I think myself that it should be expressed more broadly than Mr. Peirce expresses it." For Peirce, it seems, the meaning of a thought is the conduct it is fitted to produce. For James the meaning "can always be brought down to some particular consequence, in our future practical experience, whether active or passive; the point lying rather in the fact that the experience must be particular, than in the fact that it must be active."

After these preliminaries James devotes his address to showing how this broader expression works by applying it to the dispute between theists and materialists. At the end, however, as his last bit of trail blazing, James says that what Peirce "expressed in the form of an explicit maxim" was the "great English way of investigating a conception." The English-speaking philosophers had all been led by their sense for reality to follow this method instinctively. Over against the English philosophers James sets "the circuitous and ponderous artificialities of Kant."

The true line of philosophic progress lies . . . not so much *through* Kant as *round* him. . . . Philosophy can perfectly well outflank him. . . . May I hope, as I now conclude . . . that on this wonderful Pacific Coast . . . the principle of practicalism . . . and with it the whole English tradition in philosophy, will come to its rights, and in your hands help the rest of us in our struggle towards the light.

As we leave the lecture hall, a lawyer friend, also a member of the Philosophical Union, tells us of another trail-blazing address a year and a half ago, across the continent, at the opening of the new hall of the Boston University School of Law—an address by Oliver Wendell Holmes, Jr., called "The Path of the Law." It was promptly published in the *Harvard Law Review*. Holmes did not give his prediction theory of law a name, our friend says, but he might well have called it "legal pragmatism." It was much closer to Peirce's pragmatism than to James's practicalism.[2]

Four days later, on August 30, there is a special meeting at which Howison summarizes his own address of last May, and James then replies in detail to the criticisms that have been made of his philosophy during the past year by readers of papers before the Union. A lively but inconclusive discussion follows.

James's address appears as the leading article in the *University Chronicle* for September 1898, and then as a separate pamphlet for the Philosophical Union. The pamphlet is widely circulated by the Union and, as we soon hear, by James himself. We receive our copies and read the address we have heard. One thing that strikes us even more in the reading than it did in the hearing is James's alternation between "pragmatism" as Peirce's name for the method, and James's own much preferred "practicalism." It is "practicalism" that gets the last word, as it got the first. We gather that James uses "pragmatism" with reluctance and only out of loyalty to Peirce.

III.

Working Back

In the published address as in its oral presentation, the only reference James gives for Peirce's principle is "the *Popular Science Monthly* for January 1878." We go to the library and look it up.[3] What we find there is entitled:

ILLUSTRATIONS OF THE LOGIC OF SCIENCE.
By C. S. Peirce,
ASSISTANT IN THE UNITED STATES COAST SURVEY.
SECOND PAPER.—HOW TO MAKE OUR IDEAS CLEAR.

We have no difficulty finding the passages that James has so freely but on the whole faithfully reported.[4] Out

of context, however, they had seemed to have nothing
to do with science, and we had wondered at their appearance in a scientific journal, even a popular one. In context
we see that Peirce's pragmatism, unlike James's practicalism, is presented as an integral part of the logic of science.

We turn back to the first paper in the series, the leading
article in the volume's first issue, that of November 1877.
"Illustrations of the Logic of Science. . . . First Paper.—
The Fixation of Belief."[5] There we find the scientific
method presented as one of several ways of fixing beliefs,
contrasted with such other ways as those of tenacity, authority, and apriority. But we also find the logic of science
viewed as a second-order field of research, progress in
which depends on progress in the first-order sciences.
Each chief step in science, Peirce says, is a lesson in logic.
The most recent chief step was that taken by Darwin when
he applied to the origin of biological species the statistical
conceptions and methods first developed in political economy, for example by Malthus, and then applied to thermo-
dynamics by Clausius and Maxwell.[6]

What *was* the lesson in logic taught by this most recent
step in science? Our first guess is that what Clausius and
Maxwell had first done, and what Darwin had next done,
were illustrations of a general principle of the logic of
science: that of trying out on the still unsolved problems
of a given science the concepts and methods that have
already proven successful in one or more other sciences.
But Peirce makes no point of this beyond the single paragraph, as if in that respect these were but fresh illustrations of a lesson long since learned. It dawns on us then
that pragmatism itself is the lesson now to be drawn—or
at least a principal part of it.

Returning to the second paper, "How To Make Our
Ideas Clear," we find Peirce's pragmatism, without the
name, presented as a rule for attaining a third grade of

clearness of apprehension, beyond the clearness and distinctness of Descartes and Leibniz. The rule is: "Consider what effects, which might conceivably have practical bearings, we conceive the object of our conception to have. Then, our conception of these effects is the whole of our conception of the object."[7]

The rule seems utterly opaque at first but gradually takes on meaning from the preceding paragraphs and from the applications that follow. From what precedes we gather that the effects are sensible effects; that sensible effects are not effects on our senses but perceivable public effects of one thing on another; that practical bearings are bearings on practice, that is, on habits of action; and that these depend on desires or purposes as well as on expected sensible effects. We gather also, though Peirce does not say so, that the only way to the third grade of clearness is through the first and second.

Peirce applies the rule to such familiar concepts as hardness in mineralogy, weight and force in physics, reality and truth in logic. The point to the last two applications is that he has said in the first paper that the "fundamental hypothesis" of the scientific method is that "there are real things, whose characters are entirely independent of our opinions about them," but that "we can ascertain by reasoning how things really are, and any man, if he have sufficient experience and reason enough about it, will be led to the one true conclusion. The new conception here involved is that of reality."[8] This conception is not involved in the methods of tenacity, authority, or apriority.

We move on now to the four later papers in the series: "Third Paper.—The Doctrine of Chances"; "Fourth Paper.—The Probability of Induction"; "Fifth Paper.—The Order of Nature"; "Sixth Paper.—Deduction, Induction, and Hypothesis."[9] It soon appears that the relatively easy applications of the pragmatic rule in the second paper were

preliminary to the extremely difficult application of it
to the concept of probability, which Clausius, Maxwell,
and Darwin have so recently moved to the very center of
modern science, and which Peirce is moving to the center
of the logic of science.

In view of James's advice to bypass Kant, we are struck
by a passage in Peirce's fourth paper, "The Probability
of Induction."

Late in the last century, Immanuel Kant asked the question,
"How are synthetical judgments *a priori* possible?" . . . Not so
much by his answer to this question as by the mere asking of it,
the current philosophy of that time was shattered and destroyed,
and a new epoch in its history was begun. But before asking
that question he ought to have asked the more general one,
"How are any synthetical judgments at all possible?"[10]

In the "Illustrations" Peirce's concern is not with judgments or propositions but with reasonings. He starts from
a familiar distinction. "All our reasonings," he says, "are
of two kinds: (1) *explicative, analytic,* or *deductive;* (2)
amplifiative, synthetic, or (loosely speaking) *inductive.*"[11]
The former are said to be necessary, the latter only probable. The logic of science, as distinguished from that of
mathematics, is therefore the logic of probable reasonings.
So the logic of science must not only clarify the concept
or concepts of probability that are employed in the first-
order sciences, but must determine in what sense (or
senses) of probability the reasonings of those sciences are
called probable in the logic of science.

But Peirce goes on to subdivide those reasonings into
two kinds, which he calls induction (strictly speaking) and
hypothesis.[12] (We observe a certain discomfort about "hypothesis" and guess that sooner or later he will find a
suitable noun ending in "-duction.") He says this division
"was first made in a course of lectures by the author before
the Lowell Institute, Boston, in 1866, and was printed

in the *Proceedings of the American Academy of Arts and Sciences,* for April 9, 1867."[13] We look that up and find a paper entitled "On the Natural Classification of Arguments."[14] By dint of further searching, we find a privately printed brochure distributed at the Lowell Lectures themselves in November 1866 entitled *Memoranda Concerning the Aristotelian Syllogism.*[15] In this Peirce concludes against Kant, but without mentioning him, that

no syllogism of the second or third figure can be reduced to the first, without taking for granted an inference which can only be expressed syllogistically in that figure from which it has been reduced. . . . Hence . . . every figure involves the principle of the first figure, but the second and third figures contain other principles, besides.[16]

By dint of still further searching, we learn that the title of the Lowell Lectures was "The Logic of Science; or, Induction and Hypothesis."[17] It appears, then, that this division was Peirce's first contribution to the logic of science, that pragmatism was his second, and that the second depended on the first. And since Peirce arrived at the first by defending the Aristotelian syllogistic against Kant's essay on *The False Subtlety of the Four Syllogistic Figures,* we gather that Peirce reached pragmatism by going *through* Kant, not *round* him; and we wonder if his pragmatism may not owe something directly as well as indirectly to Kant.

Meanwhile we have noticed that the most frequently recurring technical term in the "Illustrations" is "rule." There are rules for the calculation of chances and rules for the conduct of inductive and hypothetical inference. The pragmatic principle itself is called a rule.

It finally dawns on us that what we are reading is an anti-Cartesian *Discourse on the Method of Rightly Conducting the Reason and Searching for the Truth in the Sciences.*[18] We are even tempted at first to say that Peirce's

Discourse consists of six papers because Descartes's *Discourse* had six parts. But we note references forward in the "Illustrations" to matters not discussed in subsequent papers. About the same time we notice that the publishers of the *Popular Science Monthly* are also the publishers of the International Scientific Series, and in volumes of that series published in 1878 and 1879 we find Peirce's *Illustrations of the Logic of Science* announced as one of the volumes in preparation.[19] It never appeared, and that suggests the hypothesis that he planned additional "Illustrations" for the book, if not also for the *Monthly*. The book would have come out in French and German as well as English—perhaps also in Italian and Russian.[20] The first two papers did appear in French in the *Revue Philosophique*.[21]

To learn what notice was taken of the "Illustrations" in England, we examine the library's bound volumes of the journal *Mind*. In the first four volumes (1876–79) we find a series of ten articles on philosophy in Oxford, Cambridge, Dublin, London, the Scottish universities, France, Germany, the Dutch universities, Italy, and finally the United States. This last is by G. Stanley Hall. He writes at greatest length and with greatest sympathy about Peirce, gives a summary of the six "Illustrations" so far published, and says the series is "still progressing." Its author, he says, "is a distinguished mathematician, and this discussion, in which he long ago interested himself, promises to be one of the most important of American contributions to philosophy."[22]

Wondering what the further "Illustrations" might have been, and doing some further searching among Peirce's publications, we turn up papers "On the Theory of Errors of Observation" and "The Theory of the Economy of Research" in the Coast Survey Reports for 1870 and 1876.[23] These topics seem eminently suitable. A paper on the classification of the sciences would also have been in order. We note that in the six "Illustrations" that did appear Peirce gets no further than to distinguish hypothesis and induction as forms of probable inference. We gather from the second paper that the pragmatic rule is a rule governing the admissibility of hypotheses in the first place, prior to the question which hypotheses are to be tested and in what order. A further "Illustration," therefore, might well have shown just how the rule functions, just why it is a rule of hypothetical rather than of deductive or of inductive reasoning, and just how this lesson in logic was taught by Darwin's *Origin of Species.*

Why did Peirce not finish his Discourse on Method and get it out in book form? Probably, we conclude, because in 1879 he became Lecturer in Logic at The Johns Hopkins University and had occasion there to rethink the whole undertaking in the company of the brightest, the most advanced, and the most serious students of logic anywhere in the country, perhaps in the world.[24]

We now remind ourselves that, though James made no mention of any paper but that of January 1878, he said he first heard Peirce enunciate his pragmatism "at Cambridge in the early '70's," and we wonder in what circumstances. Professor Howison tells us of a philosophical club there at that time, of which he himself and Hall became members when it was revived in 1875–76. The members "in the early '70's" included James, Peirce, Holmes, and two older men, Chauncey Wright, a scientist, and Nicholas St. John Green, a lawyer. Howison had it from James in conversation that the enunciation took the form of a paper read to that club.[25]

Though that paper was not published except as reworked later in the "Illustrations," we wonder if there were adumbrations of pragmatism in papers that Peirce did publish in the early 1870's or earlier. We succeed in locating his review article on Fraser's edition of Berkeley in the *North American Review* for October 1871. A passage catches our eyes in which Peirce says that a better rule than Berkeley's "for avoiding the deceits of language is this: Do things fulfil the same function practically? Then let them be signified by the same word. Do they not? Then let them be distinguished."[26]

Howison tells us that Peirce was an early contributor to the *Journal of Speculative Philosophy*. In the volume for 1868 we find three articles by Peirce that are even more explicitly anti-Cartesian than the "Illustrations" of a decade later.[27] In this series we are struck by the doctrine that all thought is in signs, and by the sentence:

Finally, no present actual thought (which is a mere feeling) has any meaning, any intellectual value; for this lies not in what is actually thought, but in what this thought may be connected with in representation by subsequent thoughts; so that the meaning of a thought is altogether something virtual.[28]

Shortly after that sentence, Peirce distinguishes three elements in thought and refers in a footnote to another of his 1867 American Academy papers, which turns out to be "On a New List of Categories." We find no discussion there of earlier lists, but we guess that he has chiefly Aristotle, Kant, and Hegel in mind; and his three categories remind us most of the triads in Kant's table of categories and the triadic structure of the Hegelian dialectic. We note further that both his classification of signs and his classification of inferences are explicitly grounded in his categories.[29]

Returning once more to the "Illustrations," we make two further observations. The first is that there is no mention anywhere either of signs or of categories. The second is that, nevertheless, the analyses of belief and doubt in "The Fixation of Belief" and of the three grades of clearness of apprehension in "How To Make Our Ideas Clear"

are obviously based on the categories, and that the pragmatic rule becomes fully intelligible only when we place
it and the whole of the "Illustrations" within the framework of the general theory of signs.

We conclude, therefore, that although Peirce's pragmatism did not reach print until 1878, the whole structure
in which it has so precise a place was in print by 1868,
a decade earlier; that adumbrations of the pragmatism
itself had reached print in 1868 and 1871; and that a near
approach to his full-blown pragmatism may therefore well
have been expounded in James's presence "in the early
'70's," as James seemed in his address to be saying.

It is now December 1898. We have not found the name
"pragmatism" in any of Peirce's published writings to
date. But we do not doubt that James was right in remem-
bering that Peirce was already calling his principle by
that name when James first heard him enunciate it "in the
early '70's." James's own obvious preference for "practicalism" is enough to assure us on this point. So we now
ask ourselves why Peirce preferred "pragmatism," and
what connotations it carried for him.

A teacher of ancient Greek among us says the verb
prattein meant to do regularly, to practice; the noun *pragma* the "thing" that is regularly done; the noun *praxis*
the regular doing of it; the classical adjective *praktikos*
and the postclassical adjective *pragmatikos,* concerned
with, engaged in, skilled in, devoted to, some practice
or other—for example, that of law. When Socrates is asked
what his *pragma,* his "thing," is, he understands that he
is being asked what his profession or business is.

So Peirce must have meant by the pragmatic rule the
rule that finds the third grade of clearness not in sensible
effects as such, nor even in particular actions, but in habits
of action; and not solely the habits of action of single
individuals, but those also of businesses, professions, and
communities. We note, for example, that in applying the

rule to the conception of probability involved in that of probable inference, Peirce moves first to the gambler, then to the insurance business, and finally to the un-limited community of investigators.[30] And we note further that he was already making such moves in print a decade earlier, in 1868, when he had not yet formulated the rule that governs them.[31]

We now turn to James himself. Howison has told us that James also contributed to the *Journal of Speculative Philosophy*. In its issue for January 1878, the month of Peirce's "How To Make Our Ideas Clear," we find an article by James called "Remarks on Spencer's Definition of Mind as Correspondence." Some of the characteristic themes of James's 1898 address are already there.

The organism of thought . . . is teleological through and through. . . . Far from being vouched for by the past, these [our several individual hypotheses, convictions, and beliefs] are verified only by the future. . . . The survivors constitute the right way of thinking. . . . The knower is an actor. . . . there belongs to mind . . . a spontaneity, a vote. It is in the game, and not a mere looker-on. . . . The only objective criterion of reality is coerciveness, in the long run, over thought. . . . "The fate of thought" . . . is the only unimpeachable regulative Law of Mind.[32]

Though James does not present this as a "lesson in logic" taught by Darwin's *Origin of Species,* it is evident that he too has the *Origin* very much in mind.

We find a few adumbrations in James's still earlier papers, but none as early as Peirce's, and none as close as this.[33] Between 1878 and 1898, however, we find James referring once (in 1881) to "the admirably original 'Illustrations of the Logic of Science,' by C. S. Peirce, especially the second paper," and once (in 1885) quoting the rule itself, along with the most telling preceding clause, that "there is no distinction of meaning so fine as to consist in anything but a possible difference of practice."[34]

We examine once more the dedication of the book we have been studying for a year, James's *Will to Believe*. It reads:

To
My Old Friend,
CHARLES SANDERS PEIRCE
To whose philosophic comradeship in old times
and to whose writings in more recent years
I owe more incitement and help than
I can express or repay.

A footnote toward the middle of the volume[35] now leads us to the "writings in more recent years" here meant— Peirce's *Monist* series of 1891–93, beginning with "The Architecture of Theories" and "The Doctrine of Necessity Examined." In this series we find Peirce restating,[36] revising, and supplementing the lesson in logic taught by Darwin's *Origin of Species*. He does this by developing theories of chance, continuity, and love called tychism,[37] synechism,[38] and agapism.[39] We gather, then, that James owes his pragmatism more to Peirce's "philosophic comradeship in old times" than to the published "Illustrations," but that whatever of tychism and synechism has come to him from Peirce, has come chiefly from these more recent published writings.

At last we return to Holmes. With some help from our lawyer friends, we learn that in the early 1870's he was co-editor of the *American Law Review,* that in the spring of 1872 he was University Lecturer on Jurisprudence at Harvard, and that in the July number of the *Review,* under the guise of a review of an article by Frederick Pollock, he reviewed his own lectures.[40] Already there are all the essentials of the prediction theory of law which he will state more fully a quarter of a century later (in 1897) in "The Path of the Law." In 1872 he criticizes Austin's view that command is the essence of law, that custom only becomes law by the tacit consent of the sovereign manifested by its adoption by the courts, and that before its adoption it is only a motive for decision. What more, Holmes asks, is the decision itself in relation to any future decision?

What more indeed is a statute; and in what other sense law, than that we believe that the motive which we think that it offers to the judges will prevail, and will induce them to decide a certain case in a certain way, and so shape our conduct on that anticipation? A precedent may not be followed; a statute may be emptied of its contents by construction, or may be repealed without a saving clause after we have acted on it; but we expect the reverse, and if our expectations come true, we say that we have been subject to law in the matter in hand. It must be remembered . . . that in a civilized state it is not the will of the sovereign that makes lawyers' law, even when that is its source, but what a body of subjects, namely, the judges, by whom it is enforced, *say* is his will. The judges have other motives for decision, outside their own arbitrary will, beside the commands of their sovereign. And whether those other motives are, or are not, equally compulsory, is immaterial, if they are sufficiently likely to prevail to afford a ground for prediction. The only question for the lawyer is, how will the judges act? Any motive for their action, be it constitution, statute, custom, or precedent, is worthy of consideration as one of the sources of law, in a treatise on jurisprudence. Singular motives . . . are not a ground of prediction, and are therefore not considered.

Holmes goes on in the same vein to a more extended elucidation of the concept of legal duty. He does not say that he is applying to the concepts of law and of legal duty a rule of more general applicability. He says nothing about the logic of science, but he is clearly a legal pragmatist at least, and we are tempted to say that it is as if either he was anticipating Peirce's "How To Make Our Ideas Clear" by six years, or he had heard the substance of it from Peirce's lips in club meetings. But whether in fact he learned from Peirce, or Peirce from him, or both, or neither, we cannot say.

IV.

Living Forward

The researches that have taken us back to the origins of the first period of American pragmatism have occupied the leisure of several months. It is now 1899, and we are well into the second period. Dickinson Miller has a discussion of James's address in the *Philosophical Review* for March. Friends returning from the annual meeting of the American Psychological Association at Yale University at the end of the year tell us that William Caldwell read a paper there entitled "Pragmatism." This appears in *Mind* for October 1900. Peirce himself begins using the name "pragmatism" in print in 1900.[41] In the spring 1901 issue of the Italian *Rivista filosofica* there is an article, *"Il movimento prammatistico,"* the pragmatic movement. In 1902 James has an acount of Peirce's pragmatism in his *Varieties of Religious Experience,* echoing that in his Philosophical Union address.

Also in 1902 there appears the first article on pragmatism in a philosophical dictionary. It is in the second volume of Baldwin's *Dictionary of Philosophy and Psychology.*[42] It is in five parts, two by Peirce and one each by Seth, James, and Baldwin. We are shocked to find Peirce defining pragmatism as "The opinion that metaphysics is to be largely cleared up by the application" of the now familiar rule. We take some satisfaction, however, in having guessed what Peirce now emphatically asserts, as if against James, that he "was led to the maxim by reflection upon Kant's *Critic of the Pure Reason.*" He says that James's *Will to Believe* and Philosophical Union address have "pushed this method to such extremes as must tend to give us pause." Peirce now subsumes pragmatism under the synechism which he had broached in 1868 and developed more fully in the 1890's. He even

finds a fourth grade of clearness of thought in acknowl-
edging as "ultimate good" "the development of concrete
reasonableness" and in so applying the maxim as to serve
that end.

Peirce has nearly a hundred and eighty other articles
on terms of logic in the *Dictionary.* We are curious to
learn what he has done about the term "hypothesis." Sure
enough, we find him proposing the term "abduction."[43]
That sounds not quite legitimate, and we guess that before
long he will try another "-duction" word. Meanwhile we
are prepared to find him saying that pragmatism is the
logic of abduction, but he nowhere does so.

In the spring of 1903, however, we learn that Peirce is
giving a course of lectures at Harvard University on
"Pragmatism as a Principle and Method of Right Thinking,"[44] and we are relieved to hear from friends there
that they led up to a final lecture on pragmatism as the
logic of abduction.[45] We inquire whether he presented
pragmatism also as an opinion about metaphysics and are
assured that references to metaphysics were only incidental, and no direct connection between pragmatism and
metaphysics was worked out. So we conclude that pragmatism remains for Peirce, at least in the first place, a
rule of the method for rightly conducting the reason and
searching for the truth in the sciences. We hear, however,
that there was a supplementary lecture under the auspices
of the department of mathematics on "Multitude and Continuity."[46] So perhaps there is a passage from pragmatism
to metaphysics that only a mathematician can follow.

In the fall of the same year come reports of a course
of Lowell Lectures by Peirce under the curious title,
"Some Topics of Logic Bearing on Questions Now
Vexed."[47] The topics are Peirce's three universal categories, his new system of diagrams called "existential
graphs" for studying logical relations, and his doctrines

of multitude, infinity, continuity, and chance. The first
lecture is entitled "What Makes a Reasoning Sound?" and
the last "How To Theorize." We gather that the questions
now vexed concern the nature and merits of pragmatism,
and that one of the merits of Peirce's pragmatism is that
it leads, by way of tychism, to synechism. We read Peirce's
article on synechism in Baldwin's *Dictionary*. He says it
"is not an ultimate and absolute metaphysical doctrine;
it is a regulative principle of logic, prescribing what sort
of hypotheses are fit to be entertained and examined."[48]
That puts it in the company of pragmatism. The article
on tychism in Baldwin is by John Dewey. It is based entirely on Peirce but does not say how tychism is related
to pragmatism and synechism. But if tychism, like pragmatism, is subordinate to synechism, as it seems to be,
then tychism too must, at least in the first place, be a
regulative principle of logic.[49]

In this same year (1903) two provocative books come
out: *Studies in Logical Theory* by Dewey and others at
Chicago, and *Humanism* by F. C. S. Schiller in London.
Both provoke hostile reviews. James begins to see that
there are forms of pragmatism as much broader than his
as his was broader than Peirce's. In an article, "Humanism
and Truth," in *Mind* for October 1904 James says:

since my pragmatism and this wider pragmatism are so different, and both are important enough to have different names,
I think that Mr. Schiller's proposal to call the wider pragmatism
by the name of 'humanism' is excellent and ought to be adopted.
The narrower pragmatism may still be spoken of as the 'pragmatic method.'[50]

At the end of November 1904 appears the first volume
of the *University of California Publications in Philosophy*,
with a dedication to Howison. It contains a paper by
Charles H. Rieber, "Pragmatism and the *a priori*." He
sees in Dewey and the Chicago school an "improved prag-

matism" which looks backward as well as forward for the meaning of an idea, whereas the pragmatism of Peirce and James looks only forward.[51]

In December 1904 James reprints his 1898 address in the *Journal of Philosophy*, with some abridgment.[52]

In 1905 Peirce begins a series of articles in the *Monist* explaining his own limited form of pragmatism and proposing the name "pragmaticism" for it. "Some of his friends," he says, "wished him to call it *practicism* or *practicalism*. . . . But for one who had learned philosophy out of Kant . . . *praktisch* and *pragmatisch* were as far apart as the two poles."[53] He seems to be moving by way of his existential graphs toward a proof of pragmaticism that would also be a proof of synechism, but in print he gets no further than prolegomena.[54]

In Italy by this time there is what calls itself The Florence Pragmatist Club. It publishes a pragmatist journal called *Leonardo,* with articles, discussions, reviews, and bibliographies. Papini, the editor, is a James enthusiast, but Vailati and Calderoni are Peirceans. Papini calls pragmatism a corridor theory. Vailati reviews Peirce's first *Monist* article at length and with full sympathy.[55]

In March 1907 Schiller's *Studies in Humanism* appears. He offers seven definitions of pragmatism, says humanism includes pragmatism but does not confine itself to epistemology, and remarks, without showing he has read them, that

> Mr. C. S. Peirce's articles in the *Monist* (1905) have shown that he has not disavowed the great Pragmatic principle which he launched into the world so unobtrusively nearly thirty years ago, and seemed to leave so long without a father's care.[56]

In March and April 1907 James has a two-installment "Defense of Pragmatism" in the *Popular Science Monthly.*

In June it reappears as the first two chapters of his book
Pragmatism, dedicated

> To the memory of John Stuart Mill
> from whom I first learned the
> pragmatic openness of mind
> and whom my fancy likes to picture as
> our leader
> were he alive to-day

James's pragmatism is now a theory of truth as well as of
meaning.[57] He approves Papini's corridor metaphor.[58]
He takes no account of Peirce's *Monist* articles and does
not mention pragmaticism.

At the beginning of 1908 Arthur O. Lovejoy, once a
student of Howison's here, has a two-installment article in
the *Journal of Philosophy* on "The Thirteen Pragmatisms." He does some much needed sorting out, but he
gives no sign of having read anything by Peirce.[59] And in
general, in the bewildering crescendo of articles and books
attacking and defending pragmatism in this first decade
of the twentieth century, of the few that so much as mention Peirce, nearly all do so at second hand, taking their
cues from James.[60]

In October 1908 Peirce has an article in *The Hibbert
Journal,* "A Neglected Argument for the Reality of God."
Reality, we note, not existence. Two further things strike
us. The first is that the place of "hypothesis" and "abduction" is now taken by "retroduction," and retroduction,
deduction, and induction are presented as the three stages
of inquiry. So pragmatism is now the logic of retroduction,
and "the bottom question of logical Critic" is that of the
validity of retroduction.[61] (Which reminds us that forty
years ago, in 1868, Peirce said that the question how synthetical reasoning is possible is "the lock upon the door
of philosophy.")[62]

The second thing that strikes us is that toward the end

Peirce gives an account of his pragmaticism and says: "In 1871, in a Metaphysical Club in Cambridge, Mass., I used to preach this principle as a sort of logical gospel, representing the unformulated method followed by Berkeley, and in conversation about it I called it 'Pragmatism'."[63] We are glad at last to have James's testimony confirmed by Peirce, and to have the name of the club.

About that time we hear that pragmatism was the talk of the Third International Congress of Philosophy at Heidelberg in September. The proceedings are published in 1909 and we read a paper by Josiah Royce, "The Problem of Truth in the Light of Recent Discussion," in which he calls his own philosophy Absolute Pragmatism.[64]

Royce was California's first philosopher, as well as one of her first historians and novelists.[65] Though he moved to Harvard in 1882, and the Philosophical Union was founded by Howison in 1889, Royce is a corresponding member. We all remember his own address to the Union in 1895, "The Conception of God." Some old-timers even remember that back in 1880, when Peirce's Metaphysical Club at The Johns Hopkins asked Royce for a paper, he sent them one called "On Purpose in Thought." They tell us that was the first statement of what he now calls Absolute Pragmatism. So his pragmatism, like Peirce's, James's, and Holmes's, goes back to the 1870's.[66]

Browsing further in the proceedings of the Heidelberg Congress, we find Paul Carus, editor of the *Monist,* taking part in the discussion that followed papers on pragmatism by Schiller and Armstrong. Pragmatism, says Carus, is a disease. What is true in it is not new, and what is new is false. Peirce is the only pragmatist who can think scientifically and with logical precision. The others write like novelists rather than philosophers. So Peirce has dissociated himself from them and has begun calling himself a pragmaticist.[67]

The prefatory note to the two supplementary volumes

of the *Century Dictionary* in 1909 acknowledges Dewey's assistance "in the defining of *pragmatism* and related terms." Under "pragmatic," Kant's distinction between pragmatic and practical is now clearly drawn. There is a separate article on Peirce's ˙pragmaticism. And under "pragmatism," five meanings of the term are arranged "in the order of descending generality," with illustrative quotations from Peirce, James, Schiller, and Dewey himself.

The *Popular Science Monthly* for July 1909 prints Dewey's fiftieth-anniversary lecture on Darwin's *Origin of Species*. It is full of Dewey's pragmatism, described as "the Darwinian genetic and experimental logic." It strikes us that the aptest comparison of the pragmatisms of Peirce and Dewey would take the form of comparing the lessons in logic they draw from the *Origin*. "The influence of Darwin upon philosophy," says Dewey, "resides in his having conquered the phenomena of life for the principle of transition, and thereby freed the new logic for application to mind and morals and life."[68]

James's *The Meaning of Truth* and *A Pluralistic Universe* come out in 1909. He dies in 1910. *Some Problems of Philosophy* appears posthumously in 1911 and *Essays in Radical Empiricism* in 1912. In *The Meaning of Truth* we are shocked by a footnote explaining the phrase "practical consequences": "'Practical' in the sense of *particular*, of course, not in the sense that the consequences may not be *mental* as well as physical."[69] In *Some Problems* James makes several applications of what he now calls "the pragmatic rule." But what surprises us is that, whereas his pragmatism has previously seemed to favor nominalism, he now declares for "logical realism."[70] In an appendix to *A Pluralistic Universe* there are several pages on Peirce's tychism, synechism, and agapism, in relation to Bergson's creative evolution.[71]

Royce's *The Problem of Christianity* comes out in two

volumes in May 1913. We read with particular attention the chapters on interpretation in the second volume, based on Peirce's early papers on the general theory of signs. Here for the first time, it seems to us, is a major philosopher deliberately building on Peirce's work, and building on that part of it which was the framework within which his pragmatism was later so precisely placed. In the last chapter we note the great emphasis laid upon Peirce's distinction between inductive inference (in the strict sense) as practiced in the insurance business and hypothetical inference as illustrated by Darwin's *Origin of Species*.[72]

Peirce dies in April 1914. In the latter half of July, Royce comes to Berkeley to give six summer school lectures on the process of interpretation and on communities of interpretation. These lectures are preparatory to the address he will give to the Philosophical Union on August 27 to mark its twenty-fifth anniversary. We attend the first of these introductory lectures. Royce dwells at length on the transition from his *Philosophy of Loyalty* in 1908, in which there is no mention of Peirce, to his *Problem of Christianity* in 1913, the second volume of which was worked up out of Peirce's sign theory of cognition. He says he had long known Peirce personally and been interested in his theories, but there were aspects of his theory of knowledge which he had never understood. While examining the problem of the essence of Christianity in the light of his own philosophy of loyalty, however, he was led to reread some of Peirce's early logic papers and to reconsider the way in which Peirce's earlier theories had worked themselves out in the form which some of his later writings indicated. Royce says he came then to see that Peirce's whole career as a student of logic and of scientific method was devoted to a few fairly simple and obvious ideas. He tried to restate these central ideas and found that they provided a theory of knowledge that was congenial to his own philosophy of loyalty and that provided just the key he was seeking to the essence of Christianity.[73]

Royce's able student, C. I. Lewis, is now secretary of the Union. He joined the philosophy department here in 1911. He has already addressed the Union twice himself. He introduces us to Royce after the lecture. Royce tells us that he has been taking steps toward obtaining Peirce's manuscripts from his widow for deposit in the Harvard Library, with a view to an edition of his writings.

After Royce's last preliminary lecture and the close of the summer session comes the assassination at Sarajevo and the outbreak of war in Europe. When Royce appears before the Philosophical Union on August 27, about eight hundred persons are present. The announced topic is "The Spirit of the Community." But Royce substitutes an address on war and insurance for the more general one he had originally intended. This timely address, with an added introduction and notes, is published by Macmillan in October. Royce says he wrote it after the war began and "with a longing to see how the theory of 'interpretation' which I owe to the logical studies of the late Mr. Charles Peirce, would bear the test of an application to the new problems which the war brings to our minds." In a note to the address, Royce says:

The idea, although not the name of the "Community of Interpretation," is derived by me from certain essays of the late logician, Mr. Charles Peirce. The philosophical bearing of this idea, and its relations to very deep and far-reaching philosophical issues, have been discussed in . . . my recent work entitled the "Problem of Christianity" . . . . The present application of Peirce's theory of interpretation to the philosophy of war and peace is, so far as I know, new.[74]

It does indeed appear that the application of international insurance to the prevention of war went beyond anything explicitly formulated by Peirce, but it was in the line of his moves from the gambler to the insurance company to the unlimited community.

In the following winter, Lewis hears from time to time of the acquisition and handling of the Peirce manuscripts. Our young friend Victor Lenzen, a student of Lewis's and more recently of Royce's, is sent by the Harvard department to the Peirce house near Milford, Pennsylvania. Between Christmas and the New Year, under Mrs. Peirce's supervision, he packs the manuscripts and about 1250 books in 24 large cases and ships them to Harvard.[75] Royce examines the manuscripts. At a department gathering late in March, Royce speaks of Peirce and gives some account of the manuscripts. Lenzen makes a preliminary catalogue of them. An assistant of Royce's, Fergus Kernan, is to make a selection of manuscripts to be published under Royce's direction. A former student of Royce's now at Columbia, Wendell T. Bush, coeditor of the *Journal of Philosophy*, is planning an issue of the *Journal* devoted to Peirce.[76]

That issue finally appears nearly two years later, in December, 1916, three months after Royce's own death. It begins with an article by Royce and Kernan on Peirce's leading ideas—his evolutionism, his insurance theory of induction, his tychism, his objective idealism—and on his unpublished manuscripts. It ends with a bibliography of his published writings by Morris R. Cohen. In between there is an article by Dewey, "The Pragmatism of Peirce" —much the best account so far—and articles by two of Peirce's Johns Hopkins students, Jastrow and Christine Ladd-Franklin.

As a pupil of Royce, Cohen testifies to "the frequency and generosity with which Professor Royce has, in his lectures and seminars, referred to the doctrines of Peirce." He says that James was no less indebted to Peirce for his radical empiricism than for his pragmatism. And he shows how Peirce's philosophy was grounded in his work in physics and mathematics.

For the first time we have the help of informative private letters by Peirce. Ladd-Franklin gives us three to herself and one to her husband. From one of these, late in October 1904, we glean the following: (1) further details about the Metaphysical Club in Cambridge in which "the name and doctrine of pragmatism saw the light"; (2) the way in which the "Illustrations" came to be written for the *Popular Science Monthly;* (3) the fact that "How To Make Our Ideas Clear" was written in French, though the English translation was published a year before the French original. (4) The point of Peirce's pragmatism, as distinguished from James's, "is that the meaning of a *concept* . . . lies in the manner in which it could *conceivably* modify purposive action, and *in this alone.*" (5) Royce comes closer than James to Peirce's pragmatism. "His insistence on the element of purpose in intellectual concepts is essentially the pragmatistic position." (6) "Pragmatism is one of the results of my study of the formal laws of signs, a study guided by mathematics and by the familiar facts of everyday experience and by no other science whatever. It is a maxim of logic from which issues a metaphysics very easily."[77]

We conclude that, if pragmatism survives the war and the present confusion of tongues and leaves a lasting leagacy to philosophy, it will be when the general theory of signs has been more intensively developed, and it will be because the pragmatic rule is found to be a necessary part of that general theory.

V.

Epilogue

Let us relax now from our effort of imagination and

quickly review the most relevant later developments. We entered the war. Kernan entered the army and never left it. Lenzen returned to California as a physicist and returned to Peirce only after retiring.[78] Lewis' *Survey of Symbolic Logic* with twenty-eight pages on Peirce came out in 1918 while Lewis was still in the army. In 1920 he was brought back from California to the Harvard department in the hope that he would edit the Peirce papers. He "lived with them for two years"[79] and drafted a plan but gave it up. Cohen brought out in 1923 an edition of Peirce's "Illustrations" and his *Monist* series of 1891–93, with Dewey's "The Pragmatism of Peirce" reappearing as an appendix, and with the most anti-Cartesian pages from Peirce's 1868 papers as proem. Cohen wanted to call the volume *Tychism, Agapism and Synechism,* but his wife persuaded him to make it *Chance, Love and Logic.* In an appendix to *The Meaning of Meaning* in the same year Ogden and Richards published extracts from Peirce's letters to Lady Welby which established Peirce as a founder of the general theory of signs. Six volumes of Peirce's *Collected Papers* were edited by Hartshorne and Weiss from 1931 to 1935 and two more by Burks in 1958. Cohen, out of loyalty to his teacher Royce, did more than any other single person to make that edition financially possible by raising the funds for it.

Lewis's most Peircean work, *Mind and the World-Order,* came out in 1929. He called its doctrine "conceptualistic pragmatism."[80] It was somewhere between Peirce's pragmatism and Royce's absolute pragmatism.

Dewey's most Peircean work, *Logic: The Theory of Inquiry,* appeared in 1938 after he had published reviews of the first six volumes of Peirce's *Collected Papers.* But one of the most vigorous essays he ever wrote was published eight years later, in his eighty-seventh year, on "Peirce's Theory of Linguistic Signs, Thought, and Meaning."[81]

Dewey had addressed the Philosophical Union on "Philosophy and Democracy" in 1918 and on "Context and Thought" in 1931; C. I. Lewis on "The Pragmatic Element in Knowledge" in 1926; and G. H. Mead on "A Pragmatic Theory of Truth" in 1929. Mead died in 1931. The four volumes that bear his name were all published posthumously. Dewey died in 1952, Lewis in 1964.

There are biographies of James and Dewey and editions of the letters of James and Royce. Biographies of Royce and Peirce are in preparation. A critical history of pragmatism was published by H. S. Thayer in 1968. New editions of the writings of Dewey and James are in progress. A microfiche edition of Peirce's published writings is nearly ready, and four volumes of his mathematical writings are in press. Work has begun on a new and much more comprehensive edition of his writings, in chronological order, including a large proportion of still unpublished work.

An international Peirce congress was held at Amsterdam in June 1976.

Professor Quine has been called "the last pragmatist,"[82] but if he is willing to be called one, we may be sure there are others coming on who will be no less willing.

The general theory of signs is now one of the most intensively cultivated interdisciplinary fields, and Peirce is being studied as the most original and fundamental contributor to it. But there is still no adequate account of his pragmatism within the framework he provided for it, and no adequate account of the proof he constructed for it within that framework.

Footnotes

1. *University Chronicle*, Vol. I (1898), 287–310. Reprinted, with omissions, in *Journal of Philosophy*, Vol. I (1904), 673–87. Reprinted in William James, *Collected Essays and Reviews* (New York, Longmans, Green and Co., 1920), 406–37. Reprinted in William James, *Pragmatism* (Cambridge, Harvard University Press, 1975), 257–70. In what follows I make use of the Minute Book and other records of the Philosophical Union in the University of California Archives at the Bancroft Library on the Berkeley campus, by permission of the University archivist.

2. Oliver Wendell Holmes, Jr., "The Path of the Law," *Harvard Law Review*, Vol. X (March 25, 1897), 457–78. Reprinted in his *Collected Legal Papers* (New York, Harcourt, Brace and Howe, 1920), 167–202.

3. *Popular Science Monthly*, Vol. XII (January 1878), 286–302 (hereafter cited as PSM); *Collected Papers of Charles Sanders Peirce* (8 vols., Harvard University Press, 1931–58), vol. 5, paragraphs 388–410 (hereafter such references will be in the form C.P. 5. 388–410).

4. The "open the door" illustration was contributed by James.

5. PSM, Vol. XII (1877), 1–15; CP 5.358–87.

6. PSM, Vol. XII (1877), 2–3; CP 5.364.

7. PSM, Vol. XII (1878), 293; CP 5.402.

8. PSM, Vol. XII (1877), 11–12; CP 5.384.

9. PSM, Vol. XII (1878), 604–15, 705–18; Vol. XIII (1878), 203–17, 470–82; CP 2.645–60, 669–93; 6.395–427; 2.619–44. The running head in all six papers is the series title, never that of the single paper. See note 21 below.

10. PSM, Vol. XII (1878), 717; CP 2.690.

11. PSM, Vol. XII (1878), 711; CP 2.680.

12. PSM, Vol. XIII (1878), 472; CP 2.623.

13. PSM, Vol. XIII (1878), 480n.; CP 2.641n.

14. Vol. VII (1867), 261–87 (hereafter cited as PAAAS); CP 2.461–516.

15. CP 2.792–807.

16. *Ibid.*, 2.807.

17. As announced repeatedly in the Boston *Daily Advertiser,* for example on Friday, October 19 p. 2, col. 4. The title as given on page 260 of CP 8 is erroneous.

18. Cf. Paula Rothenuerg Struhl, "Peirce's Defense of the Scientific Method," *Journal of the History of Philosophy,* Vol. XIII (1975), 481–90.

19. For example, see Alexander Bain, *Education as a Science* (New York, D. Appleton and Co., 1879), on the eighth of ten pages of announcements following page 453.

20. PSM, Vol. III (September 1873), 648. John Fiske, *Edward Livingston Youmans* (New York, D. Appleton and Co., 1894), chapter thirteen, "The International Scientific Series," 266–94 (see also 577–78).

21. Vol. VI (December 1878), 553–69; Vol. VII (January 1879), 39–57. The running head is *Peirce—La Logique de la Science,* as in PSM it was *Illustrations of the Logic of Science.* In neither journal was the title of the particular paper used as running head. See note 9 above.

22. G. Stanley Hall, "Philosophy in the United States," *Mind,* Vol. IV (January 1879) at 101–103. (In connection with "How to Make Our Ideas Clear," Hall refers to Helmholtz's treatise on physiological optics as a possible source.)

23. CP 8 p. 263, item G-1873-2(b); p. 267, item G-1879-5(c); CP 7.139–57.

24. Max H. Fisch and Jackson I. Cope, "Peirce at The Johns Hopkins" in *Studies in the Philosophy of Charles Sanders Peirce,* ed. by Philip P. Wiener and Frederick H. Young (Cambridge, Harvard University Press, 1952), 277–311, 355–60, 363–74.

25. Max H. Fisch, "Was There a Metaphysical Club in Cambridge?" in *Studies in the Philosophy of Charles Sanders Peirce,* second series, ed. by Edward C. Moore and Richard S. Robin (Amherst, University of Massachusetts Press, 1964), 3–32 at 5–7; "Philosophical Clubs in Cambridge and Boston," *Coranto* 2^1: 12–23, 1964; 2^2: 12–25, 1965; 3^1: 16–29, 1965.

26. *North American Review,* Vol. CXIII (October 1871), 449–72 at 469; CP 8.7–38 at 33.

27. "Questions Concerning Certain Faculties Claimed for Man," *Journal of Speculative Philosophy,* Vol. II (1868), 103–14 (hereafter cited as JSP); CP 5.213–63; "Some Consequences of Four Incapacities," JSP, Vol. II (1868), 140–57; CP 5.264–317; "Grounds of Validity of the Laws of Logic: Further Consequences of Four Incapacities," JSP, Vol. II (1868), 193–208; CP 5.318–57.

28. JSP, Vol. II (1868), 149; CP 5.289.

29. PAAAS, Vol. VII (1867), 287–98 at 293, 294; CP 1.545–59 at 555, 557, 558.

30. PSM, Vol. XII (1878), 609–12; CP 2.653–55.

31. JSP, Vol. II (1868), 206–208; CP 5.348–57.

32. JSP, Vol. XII (1878), 1–18 at 13, 16, 17, 18; James, *Collected Essays and Reviews,* 43–68 at 61, 65, 67, 68.

33. Maurice Baum, "The Development of James's Pragmatism prior to 1879," *Journal of Philosophy,* Vol. XXX (1933), 43–51.

34. "Reflex Action and Theism," *Unitarian Review,* Vol. XVI (1881), 389–416 at 400; *The Will to Believe* (1897), 124n.; "The Function of Cognition," *Mind,* Vol. X (1885), 27–44 at 43n.; *The Meaning of Truth* (New York, Longmans, Green and Co., 1909), 1–42 at 40n.

35. James, *Will to Believe,* 145n.

36. *Monist,* Vol. III, 183–85; CP 6.297.

37. *Monist,* Vol. II, 533; CP 6.102.

38. *Monist,* Vol. II, 534; CP 6.103.

39. *Monist,* Vol. III, 188; CP 6.302.

40. *American Law Review*, Vol. VI (July 1872), 723–25.

41. For example, in his review of the Clark University decennial volume in *Science*, n.s. Vol. XI (April 20, 1900), 620–22. Reviewing John Fiske's *Through Nature to God* in *The Nation* (69: 118) on August 10, 1899, Peirce had already spoken of James and himself as Fiske's "Pragmatist friends."

42. James Mark Baldwin (ed.), *Dictionary of Philosophy and Psychology*, II (New York, Macmillan, 1902), 321–23; CP 5.1–4.

43. Baldwin (ed.), *Dictionary*, II, 426; CP 2.774.

44. This is the title given in announcements in the *Harvard Bulletin* and *Harvard Crimson* in March, April, and May of 1903. Cf. CP 5.14–212.

45. CP 5.180–212.

46. Charles S. Peirce Papers, Houghton Library, Harvard University, Ms. 316a(s). CP 8 p. 295 at top. The lecture was announced and was given.

47. CP 8 p. 295, G-1903-2.

48. Baldwin (ed.), *Dictionary*, II, 657; CP 6.173.

49. Baldwin (ed.), *Dictionary*, II, 721.

50. *Mind*, n.s. Vol. XIII (October 1904), 458; *The Meaning of Truth*, 52f.

51. *University of California Publications in Philosophy*, Vol. I (1904), 72–91 at 73.

52. *Journal of Philosophy*, Vol. I (December 1904), 673–87. See note 1 above.

53. *Monist*, Vol. XV, 163; CP 5.412.

54. *Monist*, Vol. XV, 166f.; CP 5.415. *Monist*, Vol. XVI (October 1906), 492–546; CP 4.530–72.

55. *Leonardo*, anno III, seconda serie (Aprile 1905), 47; (Giugno–Agosto 1905), 139–40.

56. F. C. S. Schiller, *Studies in Humanism* (London, Macmillan and Co., 1907), ix–x.

57. James, *Pragmatism*, 65. "Mr. Schiller still gives to all this view of truth the name of 'Humanism,' but, for this doctrine too, the name of pragmatism seems fairly to be in the ascendant, so I will treat it under the name of pragmatism in these lectures."

58. *Ibid.*, 54.

59. *Journal of Philosophy*, Vol. V (1908), 5–12, 29–39; reprinted in Lovejoy's *The Thirteen Pragmatisms and Other Essays* (Baltimore, The Johns Hopkins Press, 1963), 1–29.

60. André Lalande, "Pragmatisme et pragmaticisme," *Revue philosophique*, Vol. LXI (1906), 121–46 is a conspicuous exception.

61. *The Hibbert Journal*, Vol. VII (October 1908), 90–112 at 103; CP 6.452–85 at 475.

62. JSP, Vol. II (1868), 206; CP 5.348.

63. *Hibbert Journal,* Vol. VII (1908), 109; CP 6.482.

64. *Bericht über den III. Internationalen Kongress für Philosophie zu Heidelberg* 1. bis 5. September 1908, hrsg. v. Th. Elsenhans (Heidelberg, 1909), 62–90. Reprinted in Royce's *William James and Other Essays on the Philosophy of Life* (New York, Macmillan, 1911), 187–254, and in *Royce's Logical Essays,* ed. by Daniel S. Robinson (Dubuque, Iowa, Wm. C. Brown Co., 1951), 63–97.

65. *California from the Conquest in 1846 to the Second Vigilance Committee in San Francisco: A Study of American Character* (Boston, Houghton Mifflin, 1886). *The Feud of Oakfield Creek: A Novel of California* (Boston, Houghton Mifflin, 1887), reprint edition with an introduction by John Clendenning (New York, Johnson Reprint Corporation, 1970).

66. Fisch and Cope, "Peirce at The Johns Hopkins," 372 (see note 24 above). Royce, *Fugitive Essays,* ed. by Loewenberg (Cambridge, Harvard University Press, 1920), 219–60; cf. 18–20, 29, 36. Correspondence between Royce and Allan Marquand in the Marquand Papers in the Princeton University Library. Minute Book of The Johns Hopkins University Metaphysical Club.

67. *Bericht* (see note 64 above), 737.

68. John Dewey, *The Influence of Darwin on Philosophy* (New York, Henry Holt and Co., 1910), 1–19 at 8–9.

69. James, *The Meaning of Truth,* 52n.

70. William James, *Some Problems of Philosophy* (New York, Longmans, Green and Co., 1911), 106.

71. William James, *A Pluralistic Universe* (New York, Longmans, Green and Co., 1909), 398–400.

72. Josiah Royce, *The Problem of Christianity* (New York, Macmillan, 1913), 394–414.

73. Royce's "First Berkeley Lecture, 1914," Harvard University Archives, Royce Papers, Vol. LXXXIV, No. 3, 5–14, quoted in Frank M. Oppenheim, "Josiah Royce's Intellectual Development: An Hypothesis," *Idealistic Studies,* Vol. VI (1976), 85–102 at 85–86.

74. *War and Insurance* (New York, Macmillan, 1914), iv–v, 50n. Here again I have used the Minute Book of the Philosophical Union (see note 1 above).

75. Victor F. Lenzen, "Reminiscences of a Mission to Milford, Pennsylvania," *Transactions of the Charles S. Peirce Society,* Vol. I (1965), 3–11.

76. See Royce's letters to Bush in *The Letters of Josiah Royce,* ed. by John Clendenning (Chicago, University of Chicago Press, 1970), 621–22 (January 13, 1915), 642–43 (February 7, 1916).

77. *Journal of Philosophy,* Vol. XIII (December 21, 1916), 718–20.

78. Max H. Fisch, "Victor F. Lenzen (1890–1975)," *Transactions of the Charles S. Peirce Society,* Vol. XI (1975), 225–26.

79. Paul Arthur Schilpp (ed.), *The Philosophy of C. I. Lewis* (La Salle, Illinois, Open Court, 1968), 16 (in Lewis' autobiography).

80. C. I. Lewis, *Mind and the World Order* (New York, C. Scribner's Sons, 1929), xi.

81. On this see Max H. Fisch, "Dewey's Critical and Historical Studies" in Jo Ann Boydston (ed.), *Guide to the Works of John Dewey* (Carbondale, Southern Illinois University Press, 1970), 306–33 at 331.

82. Ernest Gellner, "The Last Pragmatist," London *Times Literary Supplement*, July 25, 1975, 848–53.

Royce on the Concept of Self:
An Historical and Critical Perspective*

Peter Fuss

It would be understating the matter to say that Josiah Royce's position in contemporary philosophy is infirm. True, he never fails to be included in the roster of "classical" American philosophers: Jonathan Edwards, C. S. Peirce, William James, the foreign-born Alfred North Whitehead and George Santayana (who, I think, adopted us with no fewer misgivings than we have adopted them), and John Dewey.[1] But surely among these Royce is today the least read and, from the standpoint of philosophical orientation, the least liked (who, after all, would any longer wish to be associated with an unregenerate Absolutist whose intellectual roots are in, of all things, German idealism?) and thus no doubt the least influential. Recurrent "Royce revivals" seem to fizzle no sooner than they are forecast. To make things worse, the most recent spate of publications about Royce have tended in the direction of piousness—something which his earlier commentators by and large avoided. On the assumption that piety, when directed toward the truly great, is dangerous and, when bestowed on their epigoni, condemns the latter all the more quickly to oblivion, I shall try in this essay to see what can be made of a central facet of Royce's thought; and I shall do so critically, knowing that Royce himself would feel cheated with anything less.

Royce scholars are generally agreed that his thought

*I would like to mention here my indebtedness to Donald C. Williams (professor emeritus, Harvard), whose interest in American philosophy first aroused my own.

evolved through several stages.[2] My own view of the matter has been something like the following. Prior to the turn of the century, and on occasion after that, Royce construed reality to be the object of an all-embracing Absolute Mind, a "passionless eternal thought."[3] The existence of this Absolute is allegedly demonstrable in the same way that Descartes had claimed his *cogito ergo sum* to be demonstrable: by showing that to deny it is to presuppose it.[4] In contrast to this eternal Mind is the temporal order, which is real only from a finite point of view. In the conspectus of the Absolute, what is *is* from all eternity[5]—a conspectus that precludes contingency. *Human* consciousness consists of percepts and concepts whose intended objects are the same as those which constitute the content of the Absolute consciousness. For us, the criterion of truth is the agreement of *our* ideas with those of the Absolute Mind and only the latter can know whether or not there actually is such agreement.[6] Each finite individual is implicated in something beyond himself by being a unique expression of the Absolute's all-inclusive Purpose and Self. It is because of their necessary existence within the eternal Absolute, the Good as such, that the evil perpetrated by finite individuals is eternally overcome.[7]

This, aside from a number of foreshadowings, roughly characterizes Royce's position previous to 1913, when he published *The Problem of Christianity*.[8] From that time on he defined reality as the ultimate object of a Community of Interpretation consisting of an unlimited number of finite human beings. The emergence of such a community is described by Royce as an event shrouded in mystery.[9] Indeed, its continuation and existence at any time cannot be taken for granted and has an ever-uncertain future.[10] Royce here construes human knowing as a *process* whereby objects are *progressively* determined by the interpretive activity of a community of human investigators.[11] The criterion of truth is now the coherence of our perspectively limited interpretations of problematic objects with the totality of our *temporal* experience, which Royce defines as a "universe of signs" requiring interpretation. Definitive coherence is attainable only in an ideal, *final* interpretation by an *Unlimited* Community.[12] The finite individual is now implicated in something beyond himself to the extent that he becomes a *morally* autonomous member of the unlimited community of interpretation—a community which he can join only voluntarily, whose obligations only *he* can impose on himself, and whose purposes he can hamper or possibly even destroy through willful acts of disloyalty.[13]

The above two-fold sketch of Royce's philosophical development is of course a controversial one.[14] It is hard to believe that Royce's thought, at least to some extent contrary to his own intentions, underwent a fundamental transformation from a perspective in which a transcendent Absolute Self "encompasses" finite individuals to one in which finite, time-bound selves on their own initiative constitute an "unlimited community" whose eventual success in achieving an "ideally final" conspectus on human experience is postulated in a collective act of faith. But the texts that warrant this view of the matter cannot be dismissed simply by citing other texts that contradict them. In quite a different context, Hannah Arendt has written: "Such fundamental and flagrant contradictions rarely occur in a second-rate writer; in the work of the great authors they lead into the very center of their work."[15] Although I have my doubts that Royce is a truly great thinker, I am convinced that he does indeed contradict himself, and that at the center of his thought there is a rather pallid though illuminating reflection of the historical movement of thought from Kant to Hegel.

I do not think that I can justify these contentions fully

within the confines of a single paper. Nevertheless, they are inseparably intertwined, and by tracing them out here I hope to encourage a less apologetic posture on the part of Royce scholars and a less widespread tendency on the part of everyone else to ignore Royce.

II

Royce's reflections on the nature of the self can be understood only within the broader frame of his lifelong philosophical endeavor to synthesize certain elements of idealism and pragmatism which he considered ineluctable. Royce scholarship has already done much to facilitate such an understanding.[16] But if we are to arrive at a *critical estimation* of what Royce actually contributed to the concept of self—the concept he himself repeatedly identified as the central concept in modern philosophy—more work is needed. There has been insufficient study of Royce's thought within the context of the German idealist tradition which influenced him so decisively in his formative years. For more than half a century now, Anglo-American scholarship has shied away from such study, perhaps because of the notorious impenetrability of German Idealism. But without such study, we comprehend neither the scope of Royce's aims nor the reasons why he failed to achieve them. We are fortunate that Royce himself wrote extensive historical discussions of the German idealists, thus giving us an opportunity to follow his travails autobiographically. What these writings bring to light is that Royce, despite his frequently insightful account of what his German predecessors are attempting, tends to confound their quite different conceptions of the self.

Now of course Royce has been highly lauded as an interpreter of German philosophy. For instance, in a foreword to Royce's *Lectures on Modern Idealism*,[17] John E. Smith writes:

All students of that movement know how difficult it is to grasp the basic doctrines of these thinkers and, having done so, to retain enough strength to go on and address them in a critical way. The *Lectures* is truly remarkable in combining exposition with critical acumen and the book must rank among the very best in English on the line of thought that begins with Kant and ends with Hegel.

Specifically, Smith praises Royce for having resisted the temptation to opt for what many regard as the more intelligible and consistent rationalism of the British Absolute Idealists (chiefly Bradley and Bosanquet), and for allying himself instead with the "appeal to experience in the German thinkers." Professor Smith also credits Royce with anticipating some of the concerns of the current existentialists and phenomenologists by having preferred the Hegel of the *Phenomenology* to the Hegel of the *Logic*, since the former work stresses Hegel's "concern for the self and for the dialectic of experience stemming from the crucial fact of self-consciousness."[18] In what follows, I hope to indicate why these accolades were only half-deserved.

III

No doubt because his "critical philosophy" is so much more deeply and narrowly rooted in the seventeenth- and eighteenth-century controversy between the continental rationalists and the British empiricists than were the systems of his successors, Immanuel Kant has always been the most accessible of the "classical" German philosophers to the Anglo-American mind. His intensive quest for a reasonable middle ground between what he regarded as the unscientific dogmatism of the Cartesians and what he perceived to be the corrosive mathematics-and-science-destroying skepticism of David Hume led Kant to his famous "Copernican turn": the thesis that it is the human mind which determines the basic structure of our experience of the outer world, and not the other way around. While we are indeed dependent upon the external world for the so-called "matter" of sensation, this material comes to us so fragmentedly that a consistent empiricism, as Hume discovered, cannot account for the coherence of human experience. On the other hand, precisely because we do impose *our* intelligible forms upon the raw material of sensation, it is always merely the world as *we* know it, as it appears to us, that is, the "phenomenal" world that we know, never the "noumenal" world of the rationalists, the world of things as they really are in themselves. Science is capable of determining some knowledge a priori—not, of course, about the inner nature of things in themselves, but only about the universal and necessary conditions under which *we* experience things. Beyond this, nothing can be known with certainty, although if some other dimension of our experience (for example, our life as active moral agents) seems to entail transcendent realities (such as the existence of God, of freedom, and of the immortality of our own souls), then these "problematic" realities, which no science can objectively validate, may yet be objects of a reasonable faith.

Royce's own account of all this, although rather long-winded, is accurate, and his summary quite succinct:

Sense affects, apprehension beholds, sense-forms embrace, imagination, toiling as it were in the dark schematizes, categories consequently pervade the whole material of experience. There results an ordered whole, full of a transcendental affinity of fact and fact, a whole centered about the ever possible thought "It is I who think thus." This whole, always more or less ideal, a life-plan, as it were, but never a completed career for our understanding, is the realm of experience, a fruitful and well-ordered island in the ocean of ontological mysteries. [19]

Although at this point Royce taxes Kant with the familiar charge of methodological inconsistency, [20] his intention on the whole is to appreciate, not to condemn. He is above all impressed with Kant's contribution to dialectical method. In modern philosophy, Royce explains, this method is much more than an initiation rite for the impatient inquirer who would have truth delivered to him at once and entire; the inner structure of reality is itself antithetical, "so that you cannot utter a philosophical verity without giving it the form of a union or synthesis of explicitly opposed aspects or moments."[21] Thus when the "early" idealists (Royce so designates Fichte, Schelling, and the Hegel of the *Phenomenology*) made the self their cardinal philosophical principle, and their theory of self-consciousness turn on the self's radically dialectical character, they were following a path cut for them by Kant.[22] It was Kant who had been led to conclude that the self, the very subject of consciousness, is peculiarly oblivious of its own essential activity, for it keeps finding "as datum what in truth is its own deed."[23] Royce continues:

the self . . . is known to us as the one knower of experience. But whatever we concretely know, becomes, by virtue of an application of categories to sense facts, an object of experience, a phenomenon somewhere in time and in space. So soon as we try to know the self, it also becomes one of the phenomena, an empirical ego, the mere "me" of ordinary life. This empirical ego, however, is simply not the true subject, the knower, whose unity of experience is a priori and necessary. We—we as men, as various phenomena, as objects—are scattered about in our own forms of space and time, the prey of rational laws that our own transcendental unity of apperception predetermines. The self, as knower, categorizes all phenomena so that, for instance, the law of gravitation holds. Yet the empirical "me," the psycho-physical organism, falls, if that so chances, as helplessly out of the window as if his own understanding were not, according to Kant, the transcendental source of the form, and so of the laws, of all nature, including the laws which are exemplified by his own fall. [And] . . . while [the] true self, the knower, *is*, we can speak of it in no objective terms, as a real fact, without applying categories to it;

yet we know that such categories are inapplicable, since categories apply only to phenomena, and no phenomenon is the self that knows.[24]

Royce never wrote a better exegetical paragraph. What is lacking is critical distance, some sign of lingering doubt as to whether Kant helped invent, rather than merely discover, these perplexities. But Royce is in no mood to be critical at this point. Instead, sounding for all the world like Hegel, he champions the cause of dialectical philosophy in its ceaseless struggle with conventional wisdom's smugness and single-mindedness.

Common sense pretends to be free from these contradictions; but its freedom consists in a mere refusal to reflect. . . . There are two simple ways to avoid all dialectical complications. One is an easy way, viz. not to think at all. The other is a prudent way, viz. not to confess your thoughts. Philosophers scorn both ways. They try to confess their contradictions, to live through them, and so, if it may be, to get beyond them.[25]

The last portion of the last sentence just quoted sounds modest and reasonable enough until one recalls Royce's endorsement of the Idealists' conviction that antitheses, contradictions, inhabit the very heart of the real. If that is so, one might expect Royce to have been somewhat more leery of efforts to "get beyond them" than his own thought reflected. In his first major work, *The Religious Aspect of Philosophy*, Royce had proudly presented a so-called "dialectical" argument designed to show that error, which we all experience as real, is impossible unless "there is an infinite unity of conscious thought to which is present all possible truth."[26] This argument has been frequently anthologized and much discussed. But its fatal *dialectical* weakness has never, to my knowledge, been pinpointed.[27] Our consciousness of error quite possibly arises from the presence in our minds of a plurality of apparent truths that seem nonetheless to be mutually inconsistent, and their inconsistency may quite possibly be irremovable unless one avoids precisely the kind of metaphysical hypostatization which Royce's argument is designed to entrench. In other words, Royce had missed the point—or at least the force—of Kant's teaching in the Antinomies. Royce's argument assumes, it never proves, that the "space," so to speak, of truth must have a "vertical," that is, a hierarchical structure. In *The Conception of God*, published a little over a decade later (1897), Royce showed that he still had not taken Kant's lesson to heart. "The very effort to deny an absolute experience involves, then, the actual assertion of such an absolute experience."[28] What the Antinomies make clear, however, is that all one can ever derive from finite experience is what Kant called a "regressive synthesis," and that, accordingly, it makes no sense *either* to assert *or* to deny an absolute experience.

Yet in other respects Royce's critical faculties were by no means dormant. He did perceive, as we shall see next, that the biggest and most elusive fish left swimming in Kant's "ocean of ontological mysteries" was none other than the self.

IV

There is little doubt that the radical reconstruction of the concept of the *absolute* on the part of Kant's idealistic successors received its primary impetus from the unresolved tensions in Kant's own concept of *self*. As we have already seen, Kant had in fact developed fundamentally different concepts of self. First there was the empirical self or ego as object among strictly determined objects. Then there was the epistemological self, the "transcendental unity of apperception" from which the formal components of human knowledge—the sensibility's pure forms of space and time, the understanding's categories, the imagination's schemata, reason's principles—are all, as Kant had evasively expressed it, "somehow" derived. As such, Kant's epistemological self was of course much more a unifying function or principle than a person. Royce quite correctly points out that any further development of such a principle "invites a monistic formulation."[29] In addition there was Kant's ideal world of rational moral agents: free selves who in their power to initiate action somehow transcend the deterministic confines of the world of sense and empirical science, and who constitute, as Royce puts it, "a distinctly pluralistic community."[30] Now just as in Kant's theory of knowledge the transcendental unity of apperception had been the highest and widest concept, incapable of further definition just because there is no more inclusive concept to appeal to, so likewise in Kant's ethics there was no concept beyond the "problematic" notion of a kingdom of morally self-legislative rational wills. But since Kant's skepticism precluded our having knowledge of ultimate truth anyhow, Kant was able to suspend final theoretical judgment concerning the one, the other, and the relationship between them. This the Idealists were not able to abide. In Royce's words:

Thus we begin to see why, in view of the conflict between the unity of the world of truth and the pluralism of the world of action, these idealists were led to seek a solution in terms of the conception of an impersonal Absolute, which is nevertheless the ground and the source of personality.[31]

Although Royce does not attribute this formulation of the Idealistic solution to anyone in particular, it is distinctively that of Schelling, whom Royce discusses from another perspective. Before turning to Schelling, however, we would do well to consider Royce's account of Fichte, even though in *Lectures on Modern Idealism* it is brief,

rather superficial, and embedded in a lecture on Schelling. Here Fichte is credited with having "originated the
modern dialectical method." It was Fichte, according to
Royce, who first established this procedure as "the universal philosophical method," and who claimed that all con-
tradictory content is "in and of the self."[32] And it was
Fichte who, universalizing Kant's insight into the paradoxical character of the epistemologically constitutive self,
insisted that *all* action is, in one sense of the term, dialectical in nature. "It means winning one's own in a world
which is all the while viewed as foreign."[33] Royce adds
little of interest at this point. But earlier, in *The Spirit of
Modern Philosophy*, he had offered a fuller and more
critical presentation. There, after explaining that for
Fichte the entire world of experience is what the self
makes, wills, enacts in order to effectuate its moral purposes, Royce repudiates this "subjective" of "ethical"
idealism because it lacks "respect for the natural order and
for experience."[34] But what follows indicates that it is not
the subjective or ethical character of Fichte's idealism that
disturbs Royce (indeed, how else could one describe
Royce's own?), but its arbitrary character. Fichte's "true
self," Royce writes,

isn't the private person, the individual called Johann Gottlieb
Fichte, the impecunious tutor, the wavering lover of Johanna
Rahn, the professor in Jena, falsely accused of atheism. This
true self, thinks Fichte, is something infinite. It needs a whole
endless world of life to express itself in. . . . The true self is the
will, which is everywhere present in things. This will is, indeed,
the vine, whereof our wills are the branches.[35]

Here once again is the obscure but seminal suggestion that
"self" should be conceived more as a principle than as a
person. The distinction implicit here is a crucial one. In
our traditional *secular* understanding of the idea of per-
sonhood, a person's freedom and his finitude are so closely

bound together that each is thought to presuppose the other. Yet western *religious* thought has been just as strongly impelled to absolutize one "self," namely God, while nonetheless insisting that he remain a person in something like the conventional sense of that term. The resulting confusion led the German idealists gradually to reformulate, in a more dialectical way than had Aristotle and Spinoza, the idea that what is of decisive importance in and for the human self is not that it has a finite personality but that it is animated by an absolute principle.

But the distinction seems somehow to elude Royce here, just as it did in his own writings at least until the turn of the century. What Royce finds absent in Fichte instead is "any precise deduction of *how* the world of our senses, down to its very details, is an embodiment of the moral law. . . . If God's world is through and through moral, it is *also* through and through complicated, profound and physical."[36] Undoubtedly so. But having previously missed the force of a pivotal distinction, Royce now makes one that may not be there. What would a moral world, such as we might ever experience it, be if it were *not* complicated, profound, and physical? The distinctive advantage in construing the entire world as arena for our moral striving is that, in principle at least, there is nothing in such a world that can stand unexamined. It is precisely this demystification, if you will, in spite of itself, this insistence on the name of an "absolute consciousness" that *nothing* is absolutely beyond our knowing and acting consciousness, which in my opinion entitles Fichte and the other idealists not only to be taken seriously as philosophers but to be regarded as sons of the Enlightenment in their own right after all. If their skeptical fathers turn in their graves over the mysterious and mind-boggling conceptual apparatus of their children, they may find some consolation in the fact that at least the ultimate source of all these perplexities, consciousness itself, is no longer systematically inaccessible.

V

In his treatment of Schelling, Royce's emphasis is on the philosophy of nature, which he sees as providing much-needed ballast for Fichte's ego-centered approach. Nature, for Schelling, is an "objective dialectic of processes,"[37] in which later and higher stages recapitulate earlier and lower ones at a more elaborated and comprehensive level. There is an innate tendency in nature toward the evolution of subjectivity, mind. In one sense, then, Schelling might be interpreted as holding that mind is a product of nature, even while nature is an external image or symbol of self (-consciousness). Royce summarizes:

Nature is the process whereby the dialectic of the self's own life appears in outward manifestation, first as dead mechanism, but never without an union of mutually opposing forces, then as the pervasive affinity that binds nature's oppositions together, higher still, as the life of plants and animals, and at length, as the natural process whereby the human individual becomes conscious.[38]

Royce finds here a "distinctly fanciful but profound interpretation of nature as, so to speak, the external opposition of an unconscious self." But he does not expand on what he finds fanciful and what profound. Hegel, who had closely followed Schelling's scheme in his own *Phenomenology*, criticized him severely for failing to implement the poetically suggestive notions of his interpretation of nature with systematic and concrete analysis; Schelling's failure to do so may be partly what Royce has in mind when he calls it "fanciful." As for its profundity, Schelling's works, like some of Royce's own, consist largely of rather forbidding metaphysical propositions which in fact contain (at times conceal) a wealth of psychological and "existential" insights.

In particular is this true of Schelling's fascinating dialectical theology, which Royce does not examine in any detail. Had he done so, he might have thought twice about interpreting nature as the phenomenalization of an "unconscious self." For Schelling actually regards nature, indeed all reality, as the complex and tension-ridden expression of a processive, multifaceted Absolute consisting of a primal abyss as archprinciple of chaos and creativity; a dark ground of being as the source of conflict and evil in the world; and an overt personality that is open to otherness, rational, and loving.[39] Schelling sees no other way of resolving the age-old perplexities inherent in Western theodicy—or for that matter accounting for the complex nature of man. What is so suggestive about Schelling's theology—and it is just this that Royce seems to have missed—is the deeper implication of the claim that reality cannot be comprehended at all if we let stand the traditional bifurcations of mind and matter, consciousness and nature, subject and object, self and nonself. The implication, which Hegel was the first to develop with any clarity, is that selfhood or self-consciousness is inherently absolute because it embodies and expresses the principle of all-inclusiveness by its very nature: dialectically it implies or "contains" its own other.

We shall have a closer look at this when we turn to Hegel. The point to bear in mind here is that Royce, like Schelling, recurrently confused a processive, dialectical conception of consciousness with a psychologistic conception—one that virtually reduces consciousness to "the empirical ego of ordinary consciousness"[40] from which Royce himself insists "you have to abstract" in order "to form a philosophically exact conception of the self." As

Royce says in concluding his summary of Schelling's efforts:

All is the self, but the self, what is the principle at the very heart of its nature? Schelling again replies, *"The identity of its conscious and its unconscious processes."*[41]

It is a clarification of this identity, and of the terms it allegedly identifies, that Schelling fails to provide, apart from calling it, in his later work, the absolute "point of indifference." Hegel found this phase of Schelling's thought intolerably abstract and conceptually arbitrary. Royce, more charitable and less observant, recognizes Schelling's intention of affirming the identity of our conventional disjunctions in the Indifference of the Absolute, yet barely a moment later says of it: "Its root is in the unconscious, its flower is in human effort"[42]—thereby reinstating the bifurcations Schelling had wanted to overcome.

VI

Well over a third of *Lectures on Modern Idealism* is devoted to Hegel. This is as it should be: not only was Hegel the greatest of the so-called German idealists, but one or another facet of his thought, however garbled or watered down it may have become in the publicizing efforts of intellectuals, helped form the nineteenth-century mentality of which Royce was so inescapably a part. We would do well, then, to assess as best we can the quality of Royce's response to Hegel.

In his opening lecture, on Hegel's *Phenomenology*, Royce, while bemoaning the "notoriously barbarous style,"[43] commends the mode of presentation as a "remarkable union of a sensitive appreciation with a merciless critical analysis,"[44] and defends Hegel against the familiar charge of deductivism and apriorism by pointing out that the *Phenomenology* "unites logic and history rather by means of a reducing of the thinking process to pragmatic terms than by means of a false translation of real life into the abstract categories of logic."[45] Toward the end of this lecture Royce begins to touch on essential issues. Hegel, we are told,

defines in general the problem of consciousness as the problem of determining its own relation to its object. This relation cannot be determined without passing through a succession of views in which both the consciousness in question and the object of this consciousness are altered through reflection and through an experience of the problems of the situation.[46]

What we are not told is *why* Hegel holds such a view. Briefly stated, Hegel rejects the conventional notion of consciousness as something *localized* within the bounds of more or less static egos, and thus reduced to containing and expressing some "*state* of mind." Rather does he think of it as ontologically ubiquitous. Because it encompasses no specific area and is restricted to no specific experiential content, it is in principle capable of noetically assimilating any and every content. For Hegel, consciousness is inherently boundless and thus in the course of time *incapable* of resting satisfied with any *determinate* object or maintaining any one disposition relative to its object: in each instance it must negate its own stance relative to the "other" that determines it, and while doing so, by means of its recollective ability, embrace a progressively more comprehensive, more elaborately articulated whole. Further, consciousness is capable of encompassing both the knowledge of its object and the object of its knowledge. It can know whether or not its knowledge corresponds to its object because it is essentially knowledge of its own knowledge.[47] When it compares its "object-term" with its "subject-term," it is actually comparing itself with itself.

Only on this hypothesis, Hegel insists, can we account for our ability to recognize error; only on this view of consciousness can we hope to close the ever-widening epistemological gulf in *post*-Cartesian philosophy. The criterion for determining whether and when consciousness corresponds to its object falls within consciousness itself, for it is inherently self-corrective and ultimately all-inclusive. This, then, is Hegel's radical reconstruction of Kant's epistemological self, the "transcendental unity of apperception."

Dialectically inseparable from Hegel's interpretation of consciousness in terms of the impersonal is his reconstitution of this impersonal "substance" in terms of "subject," a radical extension of Descartes' idea that matter is at bottom conceptual. The only kind of objective reality that could, in principle, be fully intelligible is one capable of exhibiting in its very singularity and endless variety a universal meaning or pattern of order. This it could hardly do if it were in essence some sort of lifeless externality that could be represented adequately in, say, *mathematical* equations. Rather, nature must itself be animated by the same self-negating and self-relating principle that is operative in consciousness. This principle is *Geist*—spirit—which, according to Hegel, is alone capable of overcoming unmediated metaphysical dualisms like the Cartesian *res cogitans/res extensa* or the Kantian phenomenon/noumenon. Hegel makes this claim because his concept of *Geist* is in fact merely an elaboration of the principle of consciousness. A concrete, etymologically well-founded rendition of Hegel's *Geist* would be neither mind nor spirit but a kind of bi-gyration or double movement, just as dialectic, as he understands it, is not a more or less arbitrary sequence of assertion and counterassertion, but quite literally the ability to move conceptually in the same way as one does with two legs.[48]

According to Hegel, it makes very little difference which term we designate as consciousness and which we designate as its object (the object as it is in truth).[49] These terms (or better, moments) are so interrelated that when any sort of discrepancy arises *both* of them are altered. But if both terms of a given noetic relationship are thus in ongoing movement, the *criterion* of knowledge must move with them; otherwise it will lack all objective relevance.

Now when, in the dialectic of consciousness, something once taken to be objectively true is exposed as being merely subjectively "true," the positive insight consciousness has thus gained of the true nature of its former knowledge (its objective inadequacy) entails the negation of that alleged "knowledge" (it simply can no longer be believed); this is what *constitutes* its *experience*. What is important to note is that in this process *both* the nature of consciousness's knowledge *and* the nature of its object have been altered: as insight is gained into the radical subjectivity of its knowledge of its object, this knowledge becomes something it *knows not* to be true knowledge; at the same time it shifts its attention from an "external object" which it now knows to be a figment of its own subjectivity to an object that is itself a knowledge—hence a self-knowledge that is objective.

In his preface to the *Phenomenology*, Hegel characterized experience as follows:

Experience is the name we give to the process by which what is *immediately* apprehended in sense or thought (and is for just this reason still *abstract*, still essentially *unexperienced*) becomes alien to itself and then returns from this condition of estrangement—only *now* to be presented for the first time in its *concrete* actuality and truth as a possession of consciousness.[50]

The last phrase is potentially misleading. Hegel does not think of consciousness as some sort of substance undergoing experiential modifications. Rather, it is the dual movement of consciousness that *con*stitutes substantial objects and structures of experience even while dissolving them within its own inner dialectic.

And "precisely this unrest *is* the self."[51] Insistent as he is upon dialectical process, Hegel also shares the traditional belief that in some ultimate sense selfhood must be one and whole. The self, for Hegel, is "the *self-relating* identity and simplicity."[52] At this point it should be reasonably clear what Hegel is up to. By evenhandedly "inspiriting" mind and matter, self and substance, Hegel is seeking to desubjectify the one while deobjectifying the other, thus making their mutual interaction and processive unification possible. Only in this way, Hegel believed, could the relationship between them be demystified. Thus regarded, Hegel can be said to have brought German idealism to its consummation—by transcending it. He himself is not, in the end, so much an idealist, nor even an "objective idealist," but rather a pan-noumenalist, a philosopher for whom *nous* is equally at home everywhere.[53]

VII

And now back to Royce. His second lecture on Hegel, "Types of Individual and Social Consciousness in Hegel's *Phaenomenologie*," contains two passages which, when juxtaposed, are exceptionally revealing of Royce's strengths and weaknesses. In the first, Royce is trying to make sense of Hegel's overarching aim from a cosmological or metaphysical perspective—the lofty perch on which Royce was allegedly most at home.

The thesis to be obtained is that all being, all nature, all personal and social consciousness, are expressions of the meaning of a single Absolute, whose experience is determined by one universal or necessary ideal. This Absolute is that which is directly expressed in self-consciousness, in so far as self-consciousness is rational.[54]

This, to put it bluntly, is drivel. Hegel's contention is that there can be no such thing as philosophy unless the various moments of actuality interconnect so as to articulate themselves into a concrete universal, a whole that hangs together intelligibly. To refer to this whole—and, aside from his use of some misleading metaphors, there is no other "absolute" which survives Hegel's "merciless critical analysis"—as a *single* (what is *einzeln*, for Hegel, is always isolated, fragmentary, incomplete) *Absolute* in capital letters (nothing but the convention of capitalizing *all* German nouns warrants this usage) is simply to remystify what Hegel had so painstakingly demystified. So is to suggest that the experience of the absolute is somehow distinct from the experiences of the several consciousnesses which constitute the processual whole—and indeed to speak here of an ideal at all, never mind a universal and necessary one. Hegel strenuously insisted that philosophy's task is to describe and explicate the dense-textured fabric of what is, not the airy nebulae of what ought to be. Nor, finally, is the absolute, however one construes it, anything that Hegelian self-consciousness could ever express directly, or better, immediately. For what self-consciousness expresses at any given cultural-historical moment is always conditioned by its situation in that moment, and is therefore mediated by the perspectival limitations of that situation. The very notion of *expressing the* Absolute *immediately*, far from being rational, involves a double contradiction in terms.

In the second passage, by contrast, Royce is confining his perspective to a specific mode of consciousness which Hegel analyzes with extraordinary sensitivity: the "unhappy" (essentially Judeo-Christian) consciousness estranged from its distant God.[55]

The unhappy consciousness, then, is what James has described as the vague consciousness of being out of harmony with the higher powers, while these higher powers constitute . . . very much what James characterizes as one's subliminal self. Hegel . . . calls this . . . its own conceived and long-sought "changeless consciousness," or as he briefly puts it, "the changeless."[56]

This is insightful. The *Phenomenology* is of course studded with illustrations and analyses of sublimation, projection, and transference; but Hegel's accounts of these processes, well in advance of Freud, are in general so complex that he appears to have lost all but a handful of his readers and students—the exceptions were mostly of the calibre of a Feuerbach or a Marx. At any rate, this is perhaps as appropriate a place as any to suggest that Royce may have missed his *métier*. For the most part, he is a far better social and moral psychologist than he is a metaphysician.

Lecture 8 (Royce's third on Hegel) selectively traces the *Phenomenology*'s dialectical progression. Its high point is a short paragraph describing a section near the end of Hegel's fifth chapter.

Hegel's title . . . runs: "*Das geistige Thierreich und der Betrug, oder die Sache selbst.*" We may freely translate: "The Intellectual Animals and their Humbug; or the Service of the Cause." Few more merciless sketches of the pedantry and hypocrisy that may take on the name of objectivity and of devotion, have ever been written. For Hegel had grown up *im geistigen Thierreich* amongst the intellectual animals and he knew them to the core.[57]

Royce's translation of the title is free, but apt. Evidently Royce himself was well acquainted with the bestiary of the intellectuals, so eager to please and yet so absorbed in what they profess to be their life's work. "What they are busy in pleasing, is their own vanity. They merely call it an objective task." One can only surmise how much more palatable, and perhaps influential, Royce's *Philosophy of Loyalty* might have been had his arid homilies about devotion to ever-widening social causes been watered from time to time by critical writing like this.

Royce next points out in this lecture a much neglected dimension of Hegel's social thought. Western history has known moments when the individual was able to see his own self "writ large" in the consciousness of his community.

This his true self then assigns to the individual his private task, his true cause, gives dignity and meaning to his personal virtues, fills his heart with a patriotic ideal, and secures for him the satisfactions of his natural life. Here at last in this consciousness of a free people [a *Volk*], we have—no longer crude self-consciousness, no longer lonely seeking of impossible ideals, and no longer the centering of the world about the demands of any one individual.[58]

What is being described here is essentially the concept of self-realization as it has been articulated since antiquity by those who subscribe to the values of civic humanism or civic *virtù*.[59] Although neither Hegel nor Royce identifies the tradition by this name, Hegel repeatedly takes a nostalgic backward look at it (as Royce observes, Hegel's account of it in the *Phenomenology* comes at the beginning of Chapter Six, that is, at the very first dawning of spirit, and a similar treatment of it occurs in the *Philosophy of Right*); whereas Royce seems actually to have attempted to resuscitate it in the *Philosophy of Loyalty*. While both philosophers are unstinting in their respect for this tradition, it is the later of the two who seems far less aware of how difficult it is to recover, never mind institutionalize, such political purity of heart under modern social conditions.

VIII

The last of Royce's four lectures on Hegel, entitled "Hegel's Mature System," is by far the most penetrating and, for our purposes, the most revealing. It is here that

Royce sheds genuine light on Hegel's conception of the philosophical enterprise, comes closest to grasping that the Hegelian self is a principle rather than a person, and manages, at least for a moment, to make sense out of Hegel's absolute. I shall take up each of these points in turn.

Prefacing his remarks on Hegel's philosophical method, Royce reveals an important (in my estimation decisive) historical source of his own "argument from error." He writes that "it is of the essence of all truth to be the truth of some error, the goal which that error was seeking."[60] Royce continues:

Since each imperfect stage of consciousness is an interpretation of the whole real universe from some limited or finite point of view, and since each such interpretation is led over from its own lower stage to the next higher stage of consciousness by a process of what might be called *immanent self-criticism*—a process whereby each stage comes to a self-consciousness regarding its own purposes and its own meaning—it follows that the method of philosophy must consist in a deliberate and systematic development of this very mode of self-criticism.[61]

This is accurate; and Royce throughout his own writing sought to follow Hegel's example whenever he undertook criticism, regardless of whether his target was an intellectual position or a social institution. Such criticism is most effective when it comes as it were from within, when the critic is able to impel the consciousness he is criticizing to become conscious of, and if possible to confess, *its own* inherent limitations. This, after all, had been Hegel's primary motive in undertaking the *Phenomenology*, whose method consists in a series of empathic projections into the very marrow of limited modes of historical consciousness—projections which, when effective, enable him simply to "sit back and watch,"[62] as these modes undertake, on their own initiative, a self-interrogation regarding their limits, and in so doing set about transcending themselves.

A page later, Royce writes: "Hegel, like his predecessors, conceives the whole nature of things as due to the very *principle* which is expressed in the self. . . . the self . . . is through and through a dialectical being. It lives by transcending and even thereby including its own lower manifestations."[63] The *principle* is of course the point. Hegel did not merely claim that there is something dialectical about the activity of selves; as I pointed out earlier, he ventured one of his more striking propositions of identity in this connection: "Precisely this [dialectical] unrest *is* the self." Hegel, it will be recalled, was convinced that only by depersonalizing, desubjectivizing the living essence of selfhood as such could he overcome the unreconciled dualisms—and consequently the epistemological skepticism and the arbitrariness of metaphysical speculation—characteristic of modern philosophy. But it would seem that Royce never had more than a glimmer of what Hegel was driving at. For Royce, as I make him out, never really stopped alternately confusing and proliferating radically distinct types of self: personal and impersonal; absolute and finite; social, empirical, interpretational, and so on. Accordingly he perpetuated in his own thought the very dualisms, their skeptical consequences, and the futile attempts to conjure them away with sophistical arguments and airy systems, which Hegel had sought once and for all to overcome.[64]

As for the third point, that having to do with the "absolute," Royce rightly perceives that the strategic role of this concept in Hegel is confined to the precise manner in which he construes the relationship between whole and part. Royce's most succinct statement concerning this relationship is that "the necessary and unified totality of the phenomena is itself the absolute truth; so that there is indeed no truth to seek beyond the phenomena, while nevertheless no single phenomenon, and no finite set or circle of phenomena can constitute the truth."[65] A dozen pages later, Royce drives home the point: for Hegel there is strictly speaking neither a finite realm nor an infinite, an Absolute as such. "The infinite . . . exists only as differentiated into the totality of its finite expressions. . . . It is the totality of the finite viewed in its unity."[66] And several pages later:

the same method makes clear that no finite being and no finite truth can exist or be defined in itself, and apart from the totality of truth; while, on the other hand, the infinite being, the Absolute, which is simply the totality of dialectically organized truth, can exist only as expressed in finite form.[67]

This interpretation is, I believe, fully in keeping with Hegel's intentions. Significantly, it leaves little or no room for taking Hegel's notorious "World-historical Absolute" as anything but a dramatic metaphor, an allegorical personification of the very thing which Hegel was so concerned to depersonify: the dialectical principle of selfhood.

It seems quite obvious that Royce was unable to keep this interpretation of Hegel in clear focus. There is no indication that Royce understood Hegel's insistence upon equating his absolute-as-totality with the impersonal and ubiquitous principle of selfhood. And once again, Royce's capitalization should arouse one's suspicions. These suspicions are confirmed, I regret to say, by the two paragraphs which immediately follow, the second of which concludes Royce's account of Hegel in this book. (I quote it in full, with my own comments interspersed:)

The philosophical and the religious consciousness, phenomenally, exist as events in time. They are expressions, however, of a process which must be viewed not as temporal but as eternal [this after just having finished explaining that the process is strictly speaking neither since it is in fact both]. In human philosophy and in human religion, the Absolute [capitalized once more] temporally appears as being at a certain moment what he [note the personification] in fact timelessly is, conscious of himself. For in the Absolute all the dialectical stages which time separates, are eternally present together [precisely the kind of transcendental consolation, useful when addressing Rotarians and ladies clubs, which Hegel found so delusory and, from a philosophical point of view, so repugnant].[68]

IX

There is a concluding lecture, "Later Problems of Idealism and its Present Position," in which Royce's distinctive shortcomings and strengths as proponent of this viewpoint are once more clearly in evidence. First we encounter the doctrinal warrior, brandishing more of the kind of polemical weapons which had first appeared in *The Religious Aspect of Philosophy*. A contemporary moral educator, it seems, had tried to argue that realism—"a faith in the real world as being something independent of the minds of us fallible mortals, is the only wholesome doctrine, the only corrective of the intellectual excesses of youth, the only safeguard against visionary and possibly morbid waywardness.'[69]

These, Royce acknowledges, "are robust ideals unquestionably; but the man who interprets his world in terms of them is a philosophical idealist, although it is part of his creed that he must not admit this fact even to himself."[70] Royce here draws on Hegel's description of the power of the Enlightenment for an analogy:

Modern idealism, like that former rationalism, is a sort of universal and often secret infection. Whoever contends against it shows that he is already its victim. . . . By virtue of his very reasoning he confesses that the question, "How ought I to conceive the real?" is logically prior to the question, "What is the real itself?"

But as Hegel knew better, pseudo-dialectical arguments like this don't work; they are static and sterile—at bottom because they are not in truth dialectical. They stand on one leg of a fashionable but futile controversy, insist that someone perched on the other leg cannot walk thus, and overlook the simple fact that it is the same for them both. If Royce had read more carefully the section of the *Phenomenology* to which he is alluding,[71] he would have realized that Enlightenment carries the day against its antagonist, Faith, only when it manages, after a long phase of self-deception, to uncover the authentic moment of faith within its own consciousness. The same of course is true of "idealism" and "realism."

In all fairness to Royce, he is by no means always entirely unaware of this. It is the quality and consistency of his awareness that troubles me. In a characteristically elusive, slippery passage we are told:

Philosophy must indeed criticize as thoroughly as it is able the various tests that we actually use, the various faiths upon which men act, the Protean forms of the sentiment of rationality. What I insist upon is that such criticism must itself in the long run be guided by a conscious rational ideal, which when it becomes conscious must appear as the ideal of our own intelligence, of *the self that speaks through us*, of the reason of which we are the embodiment.[72]

What, exactly, does this say? If it maintains that the inherent and latent rationality within us must be made manifest in ourselves and in our world before we can find fulfillment as rational beings, fine. If it further implies that this undeveloped capacity appears to us as a more or less alien ideal until it is concretely actualized, all well and good. And if the italicized words are intended to remind us that etymologically "person"—that is, *per-son-(a)*—derives from what has the power to speak immortal words through the mask of the stage actor's fleeting singularity, then Royce is to be commended for his erudition. But if, as I very much suspect, Royce is once again hypostatizing a transcendent Absolute, then he has not appreciated the critical thrust of Hegel's dialectic of enlightenment—namely, that to fixate God, the Absolute, or the Self (in capital letters) anywhere outside or beyond ourselves is to falsify our relation to ourselves by entrenching us ever more firmly in our own finitude.

Several pages later, however, we encounter a quite different Royce. Now he is championing the cause of individuality, and in the process articulating what, for him, is a remarkably fluid conception of the nature of philosophy. Empirical science, he argues, aims at intersubjective confirmation, concerned, as it is and should be, with what our experiences have in common. But the price exacted by this emphasis is individuality. All individuals are,

as Leibnitz said, mirrors of the universe. But since the universe is . . . just the system of living mirrors itself, what is common to the various world-pictures is never the whole truth. Hence it is of the nature of a philosophy always to be in the presence of problems which forbid a final systematic formulation from the point of view of the individual philosopher, just because these problems are soluble only from the point of view of other individuals. Philosophy . . . is therefore much less able than are the empirical sciences to define a settled result upon which further investigation may be based. . . .

Thus everything in philosophy is properly subject to reinterpretation from new points of view. . . . For countless individual interpretations have not yet been made, or are not now in synthesis. . . . It is the value and not the defect of philosophy that it proceeds not by mere accumulation of settled discoveries, but by a constant re-interpretation of the meaning of life.[73]

In retrospect this passage probably does the empirical scientist too little justice and the philosopher too much. But it is impressive nonetheless. For once affirming the inescapable reality of individuals in a way that Hegel himself had never been able to do without equivocation, Royce perceives what this implies regarding the very enterprise of philosophy, namely, that it is inherently defeasible. Commenting on this passage in an editorial footnote, Jacob Loewenberg wrote: "In this whole discussion are foreshadowed some elements of the later theory of interpretation as expounded in *The Problem of Christianity*." That is so. In this his last major work, Royce had credited a rereading of C. S. Peirce's essays on interpretation with having inspired his own reformulations. Royce might have added that Peirce's "contrite fallibilism" had in the meantime been working its salutary influence on our American idealist's sensibility as well.

X

In the preceding I have tried to show that Royce, in spite of his affinity with the unfolding of German philosophy from Kant to Hegel, only half understood it. I have paid closest attention to Royce's reading of Hegel, for I think I detect there a general tendency on Royce's part to continue looking for some kind of absolute, all-inclusive self after it has already been found. It had been Hegel's contention that selfhood or its principle, consciousness, wherever it is present, is implicitly and inherently ubiquitous and all-encompassing. Accordingly, even when such selfhood or consciousness is embodied in finite beings, there is no need to look beyond them to some transcendent entity that synthesizes their limited perspectives and overcomes their finitude. But as I have tried to show, Royce's imperfect grasp of all this led him to keep postulating such a transcendence after all and then passing it off as Hegel's own view.[74] In the end the key to Royce's difficulties is to be found in his externalistic and reductionistic use of dialectical method. For Hegel, dialectic is a process

by which ostensibly finite and fragmentary modes of consciousness—as often as not defiantly entrenched islands
of immature selfhood—enter into confrontations which
lay bare not only their deficiencies but their limitless
inner capacity to absorb and embrace what they encounter
and thus eventually to make their latent wholeness manifest. In Royce's hands dialectic becomes a method of
argumentation by which irretrievably finite and fragmentary conscious entities are so fixated within their limitations that nothing but a *deus ex metaphysicis* can redeem
them. And indeed once these entities have been denied
their inherent powers of self-correction and self-transcen-
dence, the appeal to an outside agency—the Roycean
Absolute in one or another of *his* guises—is as humanly
understandable as it is, philosophically speaking, an act
of desperation.

In concluding, I would like to venture the opinion that
Royce's final recasting of his thought in the form of his
theory of interpretation, for all of this theory's freshness
and attractiveness, suffers from precisely the same faulty
notion of dialectic which had undermined his earlier efforts. Since I have discussed Royce's theory of interpretation extensively elsewhere,[75] I shall presume general
familiarity with it here and confine myself to several critical observations.

Notice, to begin with, how Royce establishes his theory
of interpretation. Apparently taking his cue from Kant's
famous dictum that concepts without intuitions are empty,
whereas intuitions without concepts are blind, Royce defines perception and conception as "self-limiting" and
isolated mental states, the one "lonesome" and the other
"sterile." Conceived in this reductionistic way, they have
nothing in common and, if left to their own devices, never
interpenetrate and never yield coherent knowledge.[76]
Royce thereupon introduces interpretation as an inher-

ently unlimited "social" process which mediates the other two defective modes of knowledge and thus saves them from their own futility. But a doctrine of this sort is itself futile. Because Royce begins with two impoverished terms, each and both together incapable of dialectical self-development, his salvific third term remains external to them. Indeed, it is difficult to see by what dialectical sleight of hand a dynamic, living relationship could be mediated between admittedly static and dead terms.

As Royce proceeds to develop his doctrine of interpretation, he tends to leave perception and conception behind altogether, preferring to analyze all problematic situations in terms of a triadic relationship involving interpreter, sign to be interpreted, and interpretee. But by his own insistence, once an interpretative process is under way, these terms (myself as problematic object to myself, you and I attempting to establish some common ground for interpersonal communication, we in concert seeking to make sense of the world of objects we experience inter-subjectively) tend to exchange roles. And by his own admission there is then room for a potentially infinite number of interpretative acts *between* any two of the terms in question. It may well be the inescapable logic of this proliferation that accounts for the relative open-endedness of Royce's later doctrine—an open-endedness which retrospectively reinforces his insistence on the defeasibility of our necessarily individualistic philosophies in *Lectures on Modern Idealism*. But the price exacted by this apparent dilution of his earlier absolutism is high. He has now committed himself to what Hegel criticized as a defective, merely quantitative infinite: an infinite regression very much like the "third man" perplexity that had already beset Plato in the *Parmenides*.[77]

Royce is unlikely to have been unaware of all this, that is, to have rested content in the illusion that a Roycean "infinite series," interpretational or otherwise, could meet the demands of the Hegelian "concrete universal." It is for this very reason, I think, that we find in *The Problem of Christianity* the strategic reappearance of the Absolute Self or God as "Infinite Interpreter," unaccompanied by any clear suggestion that a transcendent entity thus conceived is to be understood metaphorically. Although armed with inferior conceptual tools, Royce was after all constitutionally no more able than Hegel to leave dualisms unreconciled, gaps unbreached, infinities unconcretized.

A decade ago in an appendix to my book on Royce, and again earlier in this essay, I construed the evolution of Royce's thought in such a way as to suggest that he may have abandoned his absolutism in his last years. In both instances I did so quite aware that Royce made some statements that seem to support, but on the whole, more that seem to militate against such an interpretation. For my concern was then, as it is now, with the "inner logic" of Royce's intellectual development, a logic of whose exigencies one need not assume Royce to have been entirely conscious. I now regard this suggestion as sufficiently misleading to require retraction.[78] It was not that Royce abandoned, or perhaps even significantly emasculated, the Absolute. He was far too unregenerate a transcendentalist to do that. Rather, he sensed the inherent dangers in an unqualified immanentism such as Hegel seems at times to espouse—even while he was determined to hold idealism to its commitment to the concrete (in Royce's own language: to its inalienable pragmatic orientation). Royce wanted nothing more than to concretize his Absolute, to reconcile rather than to have to opt between the finite and whatever may or must lie beyond. But his grasp of the Hegelian concept whereby such a reconciliation could in principle be effected was too infirm, and so he fell back into the antinomies I have pointed out above. This relapse is what invites the unhappy conclusion that Royce, for all of his undeniable philosophical talents and virtues, may well be a roadblock in the development of an indigenous American philosophy. For although chronologically he comes well after Hegel, the textual evidence indicates that he never in fact caught up.

I do not wish to be unfair. Royce is merely one of a number who tried and failed. In the sincere hope of being persuaded otherwise, my general impression is that, in spite of some auspicious beginnings,[79] American philosophy has yet to happen.

Footnotes

1. Conveners of symposia and writers of anthologies on American philosophy differ over the wisdom of updating such a list. Those with a predilection for keeping abreast tend by this time to have reached W. V. Quine, whereas the traditionalists, as one might expect, not only prefer the authors of their classics to be safely dead, but can sometimes be induced to confess, at least in private, that for them Quinine logic is and remains a bitter pill. (Someone else said this, I should hasten to acknowledge; Quine tells me it was Harry Sheffer, back in the 1930's.)

2. The story has been told more than once, with variation in detail, disagreement regarding the number and dating of phases, and some controversy over where it all ended. As the first half of this section will reflect, I find myself still attracted to W. H. Werkmeister's version of this story. See Werkmeister, *Philosophical Ideas in America* (New York, Ronald Press, 1949), the ninth chapter of which is devoted to Royce.

3. Josiah Royce, *The Religious Aspect of Philosophy* (New York, Houghton Mifflin, 1885), 370 and *passim*. For a slightly fuller account of this intellectual development, see my *The Moral Philosophy of Josiah Royce* (Cambridge, Harvard University Press, 1965), 259–63 (Hereafter cited as *MPJR*).

4. Royce, *Religious Aspect*, 384–435.

5. *Ibid.*, 465.

6. *Ibid.*, 371; cf. Josiah Royce, *The World and the Individual* (New York, Macmillan, 1899), I, lectures 7 and 8.

7. Royce, *The World and the Individual*, II, lectures 8 and 9.

8. Royce's absolutism does have a more voluntaristic cast in *The World and the Individual* than it had in *The Religious Aspect of*

Philosophy. But this difference would appear to be far less decisive than that reflected in *The Problem of Christianity.*

9. Josiah Royce, *The Problem of Christianity* (New York, Macmillan, 1913), I, 183–85; II, 101–102.

10. *Ibid.*, II, 37ff.

11. *Ibid.*, II, 267ff.

12. *Ibid.*, II, 290, 323ff.; cf. *Royce's Logical Essays*, ed. by Daniel S. Robinson (Dubuque, Iowa, W. C. Brown, 1951), 118–24.

13. Royce, *Problem of Christianity*, II, 388 and *passim.*

14. It, or rather its 1965 forebear, has recently been disputed at some length. See David L. Miller, "Josiah Royce and George H. Mead on the Nature of the Self" in *Transactions of the C. S. Peirce Society*, Vol. XI, No. 2 (spring 1975), 68–89. I shall have something further to say about this controversy in the conclusion.

15. *The Human Condition* (Chicago, University of Chicago Press, 1958), 104–105, where Karl Marx's highly equivocal conception of labor is being examined.

16. To mention several of the more recent works: John E. Smith, *Royce's Social Infinite* (New York, Liberal Arts Press, 1950); J. Harry Cotton, *Royce on the Human Self* (Cambridge, Harvard University Press, 1954); J. Loewenberg, *Royce's Synoptic Vision* (Baltimore, Johns Hopkins University, 1955); W. E. Hocking, "On Royce's Empiricism" in *The Journal of Philosophy* (1956); and my *MPJR* (1965).

17. First delivered at Johns Hopkins in 1906, these lectures were edited and published posthumously by J. Loewenberg in 1919, and reprinted by Yale University Press with a new foreword by Professor Smith in 1964. Cf. Royce, *The Spirit of Modern Philosophy* (Boston, Houghton Mifflin, 1892), a broader and less technical study of German thought, regarded by many as his best work stylistically.

18. Royce, *Lectures on Modern Idealism*, viii (hereafter cited as LMI). In his editor's preface J. Loewenberg had already praised Royce for avoiding the obvious by finding in the early Schelling "the pulse of the dialectical method, and in the *Phenomenology* rather than in the *Logic* . . . the soul of Hegel," xii.

19. *Ibid.*, 57–58. This formulation was inserted by the editor and taken from an unpublished fragment entitled "Some Characteristics of Being." Compare Royce's account in *The Spirit of Modern Philosophy* (New York, George Braziller, 1955), Lecture IV, 101–34, and Appendix B, 482–91.

20. ". . . the circle is that, in order to reach his epistemology . . . one has to accept his ontology, while after one has accepted the epistemology, anything but a wholly problematic ontology is excluded" (LMI, 61).

21. *Ibid.*, 88.

22. *Ibid.*, 90.

23. *Ibid.*, 91.
24. *Ibid.*, 91–92.
25. *Ibid.*, 93–94.
26. Page 346 (in italics) and *passim*.
27. Cf. my review of *The Basic Writings of Josiah Royce* in *Journal of the History of Philosophy*, Vol. XI, No. 2 (April 1973), 284–85.
28. Page 380.
29. *LMI*, 72.
30. *Ibid.*, 71. There is, on top of that, the implication of Kant's *Critique of Judgment* that there may be an "esthetic" self whose relationship to the world of nature is different, both in its constitutive power and in its receptive capacity, from the empirical, the epistemological, or the moral self. But Royce takes no note of this, and I cannot pursue the matter here.
31. *Ibid.*, 72.
32. *Ibid.*, 96–98.
33. *Ibid.*, 99.
34. Pages, 152–55.
35. *Ibid.*, 159.
36. *Ibid.*, 166.
37. *LMI*, 102.
38. *Ibid.*, 104.
39. So far as I am aware, no adequate account of this—by Schelling himself or by anyone else—is available. The best we have is his 1809 essay *Philosophische Untersuchungen über das Wesen der Menschlichen Freiheit und die damit Zusammenhängenden Gegenstände*, whose English translation (not a very good one) is entitled simply *Of Human Freedom* (La Salle, Illinois, Open Court, 1936).
40. *LMI*, 105.
41. *Ibid.*, 133.
42. *Ibid.*
43. *Ibid.*, 136.
44. *Ibid.*, 151.
45. *Ibid.*, 145.
46. *Ibid.*, 156.
47. Cf. Georg Wilhelm Friedrich Hegel, *The Phenomenology of Mind*, trans. by J. B. Baillie, rev. ed. (New York, Harper Torchbooks, 1967), 140. The German edition from which I am making my own retranslations here is *Phänomenologie des Geistes*, sechste Auflage (Felix Meiner, 1952), 72 (henceforth cited as, first Meiner, then Baillie).
48. See the forthcoming translation of, lexicon for, and commentary on Hegel's *Phenomenology* by Peter Fuss and John Dobbins. *Geist* and *Begierde*, whose connotation for Hegel is de-sire (=bi-gyration), have substantially the same etymological connotation.
49. Meiner, 71ff; Baillie, 140ff.

50. Meiner, 32; Baillie, 96 (italics mine).

51. Meiner, 22; Baillie, 83 (italics mine again).

52. Meiner, 22; Baillie, 84 (and once more).

53. It is this pan-noumenalism—whose validity Hegel knows he must presuppose as well as seek to illustrate and justify in detail—which motivates the intricate play of conceptual identifications found in his *Logic*.

54. *LMI*, 167.

55. Hegel, *Phenomenology*, chapter four, B, the last portion of which Royce himself translated and entitled "The Contrite Consciousness." The selection is to be found in Benjamin Rand, *Modern Classical Philosophers* (Boston, Houghton Mifflin, 1924), 614–28.

56. *LMI*, 181.

57. *Ibid.*, 199.

58. *Ibid.*, 200.

59. For a most illuminating study of this tradition in its Greek, Italian, and Anglo-American manifestations, see J. G. A. Pocock's recently published *The Machiavellian Moment* (Princeton, Princeton University Press, 1975).

60. *Ibid.*, 217–18.

61. *Ibid.*, 218 (italics mine).

62. Hegel, *Phenomenology*, introduction and *passim*.

63. *LMI*, 219 (italics mine).

64. The extremely complicated question regarding the extent to which Hegel himself succeeded cannot be pursued in this essay. See my forthcoming "Theory and Practice in Hegel and Marx: An Unfinished Dialogue."

65. *LMI*, 215.

66. *Ibid.*, 227.

67. *Ibid.*, 230.

68. *Ibid.*, 231.

69. *Ibid.*, 236.

70. *Ibid.*, 237.

71. Hegel, *Phenomenology*, chapter six, B, II.

72. *LMI*, 239–40 (italics mine).

73. *Ibid.*, 243–45. Cf. *MPJR*, 86–93.

74. This tendency is even more pronounced in the earlier *Spirit of Modern Philosophy*, 204–16, than in *LMI*.

75. See my *MPJR*, chapter five and *passim*, and "Interpretation: Towards a Roycean Political Philosophy" in *Revue Internationale de Philosophie*, No. 79–80 (1967), 120–31.

76. Cf. Royce, *The Problem of Christianity*, II, 149–51.

77. Most instructive in this connection is the semischolarly appendix on Kant in Royce, *The Spirit of Modern Philosophy*, in particular pages 484–89. Royce there accepts uncritically not only Adickes' "patch-

work theory" of how Kant's *Critique* must have been composed, but Vaihinger's "objective subjectivity" thesis as well, apparently not realizing that the latter likewise succumbs to the "third man" argument: between the Kantian thing-in-itself and the human subject one thus opens the door to an unlimited number of relative things-in-themselves.

78. The latest to have been misled—to the point of supposing that I ever thought Royce at any time deliberately embraced some form of "naturalism"—is David L. Miller. See note 14.

79. To mention a few: Jonathan Edwards rethinks Berkeley in a teen-age trance, then later demonstrates conclusively that whatever it may be wherein our vaunted freedom consists, it cannot possibly be our wills as such. Peirce, recovered from the shallow instrumentalism of "How to Make Our Ideas Clear," seeks a conceptual ground for modern science in, of all places, Scotistic Realism. Royce helps inspire the still-emergent science of hermeneutics with his theory of interpretation, itself inspired by Peirce. James attempts a concrete phenomenology of the religious consciousness just at the point when post-Hegelian phenomenology on the Continent is about to become hopelessly scholastic. Dewey, Whitehead, and Santayana, each in his own way, experiments with ways of widening empirical habits of mind which, had they only cultivated them more consistently, might have deflected several generations of positivists, analysts, and metalanguage maniacs from the hopelessness of *their* scholasticism.

George Santayana and the Idea of Philosophy

Frederick A. Olafson

Welcome as it is, the inclusion of Santayana's name in the roster of American philosophers we are to consider on this occasion immediately raises a difficult question: what place, if any, does Santayana have in a distinctively American philosophical tradition? He did not after all regard himself as being an American but rather as a foreigner who had lived for many years in the United States; and of course the last forty years of his life, like the first eight, were spent in Europe. In matters of spiritual citizenship as well, Santayana repeatedly declared his independence of and lack of sympathetic affinity for the American philosophical and intellectual tradition; and if he was educated at the Bostin Latin School and Harvard College, it was to Spinoza and Lucretius that he looked for his models of philosophical distinction and for that detachment of mind which he found so deplorably lacking in the busy citadels of American intellectual commerce. Although his name has often been coupled with those of Royce and James as the giants of philosophy during Harvard's Golden Age, the truth is that Santayana has always figured as a kind of exotic within American philosophy. It was not just that he was a Spaniard and a Catholic in a social and intellectual milieu that was still predominantly Anglo-Saxon and importantly influenced by the Puritan heritage. There was also the fact that he wrote much more gracefully and fluently than is usually expected of a serious thinker; and beyond that he fastidiously avoided any direct participation in the philosophical undertakings of his time, preferring instead the isolated posture and unfashionable range of interests of an ancient sage. It is true that, during the period of realism and naturalism in American philosophy, the name of Santayana was often cited together with those of Whitehead and Dewey as representing an intellectual movement of wide influence and appeal. That species of naturalism has, however, long since given way to others that recognize no bond of indebtedness to Santayana, and these days one can scarcely discern any signs of interest among currently active philosophers in Santayana's *oeuvre*. The conclusion that is forced on us is very like the one reflected in Santayana's own self-description, and we must ask what this alien figure with his studied distaste for the dominant temper of the American philosophical community is doing here in the company of the most distinguished representatives of a tradition to which he addressed so many ironic rebukes.

Although I do not propose to make the attempt here, I think that it might be possible to meet this line of argument on its own ground and to show persuasively that Santayana's thought had a closer and more organic relationship to the philosophical milieu within which it came to maturity in such an apparently independent way. It seems clear, for example, that for all his proud Latinity there is no discernible tincture of Spanish influence in Santayana's philosophy; and it further suggests itself that, just as the art of Henry James—another longtime resident in Europe—remained indefeasibly a commentary on the American scene, so Santayana's thought might be interpreted as standing in a kind of contrapuntal relationship to the dominant line of American philosophical activity. Whatever the validity of this broader interpretation might prove to be, however, there is at least one respect in which the bearing of Santayana's thought on the American philosophical tradition is beyond question. I have in mind the fact that he was almost as much a philosophical critic as he was an original philosopher and that among the philosophers who are dealt with in this book he was the only one who attempted a broad critical characterization of the achievements and ethos of American philosophy.[1] This aspect of Santayana's thought will be the focal one for the present discussion. More specifically I want to concentrate on what Santayana has to say about the broader understandings that have defined the goals of philosophical activity in this country rather than on particular philosophical doctrines. In the course of this discussion, Santayana's treatments of such American philosophers as Royce and James will be considered as well as of the broader tendencies of thought that found expression in their work. At the same time, however, I propose to consider in what measure Santayana's own philosophy may be said to exemplify the idea of philosophy that he uses to appraise other philosophers; and here I will express some reservations of my own with respect to the kind of naturalism that Santayana defended.

I.

To quite a remarkable extent American philosophy has been the product of the New England mind; and if an external observer in the nineteenth century, whether from Mars or from Avila, had been deciding on the right point of vantage from which to carry on his inquiries into the state of the American mind there can be no doubt that Boston and Cambridge would have been the uniquely right places for him to land as, of course, Santayana very presciently did. In his novel, *The Last Puritan,* written long after he had left America for Europe, he has given us a remarkable portrait of a personality in which some of the most deeply ingrained characteristics of the Puritan spirit survive at a time when they had become historical curiosities in the expanding America of the twentieth century. Among those attributes none was more fundamental than the Puritan's overriding sense of moral urgency, the conviction that his life formed part of a great moral enterprise which had been set in motion in the world and to which, as the ultimate standard of seriousness and worth, all the particulars of secular life were to be referred for a determination of their claims upon him. In its original form this conviction has been explicitly doctrinal and theological; and there was no hesitation on the part of Puritan divines about treating vast sectors of secular life as having at best a marginal contribution to make to the grand moral design and quite possibly only the kind of negative contribution that was a necessary condition for the moral chiaroscuro of the Puritan world view. But as the prospects and opportunities of life in the new world grew steadily more positive and as the material comforts of life multiplied, it proved impossible to maintain a view of the secular world that was as grimly restrictive and censorious as that of the first Puritans; and a transition began to the more liberal forms of protestantism with their less exacting conditions for incorporating much of the substance of actual social life into the great enterprise of salvation. What was not surrendered, however, was the insistence that the scene of human life be viewed from the standpoint of its ultimate moral significance. In America, as in Europe, philosophical idealism proved to be the ideally suitable instrument for carrying out this task of accommodating the vast bulk of what the new history and the still newer science were bringing to light while associating it with a sense of a spiritual progression. It was this same idealism that dominated the philosophical world during most of Santayana's career as a professional philosopher; and it is hardly surprising, therefore, that so much of his criticism of the way in which philosophy was understood and practiced in this country took the form of a decidedly negative commentary on the principal doctrines as well as the underlying cultural ethos of idealism.

On many occasions Santayana expressed the opinion that the essential insights of philosophy could be reached through a kind of natural shrewdness and honesty and without benefit of much, if anything, in the way of technical apparatus. These insights had to do with man's situation within and ultimate dependency upon nature—the "realm of matter" as Santayana called it later—and it was his view that the rational conduct of life must rest upon an acceptance of these truths and especially upon the ability to distinguish the ideal from the real, to the prejudice of neither, which they make possible. There was thus an important sense in which the truth which philosophy has to communicate in its formal idiom was a restatement of what we would already be in a position to grasp if it were not for the thousand influences that seek to conceal this same truth from us. In Santayana's view, these influences were very strong within both the social and the intellectual worlds of nineteenth-century America and they derived principally from that profound moralization of all facets of the human experience that had survived the dilution of the religious dogmas with which it had originally been associated. Their effect was to force philosophers into complicity in what was finally an exercise in mystification: the effort to hold erect the one indispensable tenet on which the moral vision of the world depends. This was the postulate of a congruence between the moral impulse in man with a moral and teleological principle of organization within the world process itself. Through its effort to support the fiction of such a congruence or, at any rate, to keep it from being too

nakedly exposed for what it was, philosophy became a
work of edification, an effort to force the stubborn facts
with which our natural existence inescapably acquaints
us into harmonious syntheses of varying degrees of im-
plausibility. In the case of his principal, and certainly
most distinguished, contemporaries—Royce and especially James—there was of course a very real critical distance from the cruder forms of this orthodoxy, and this
distance was no doubt responsible for a certain wistfulness
and even sadness that Santayana sometimes noted in
these otherwise so energetic representatives of American
thought. But if they were unable to embrace the hypothesis
of a providential ordering of the affairs of this world
in any of its simpler and more familiar forms, they were,
in Santayana's view, equally unable to liberate themselves
from its influence. As a result, their philosophies were
lacking in that supreme virtue of speculative thought to
which Santayana recurs again and again: disinterestedness. As Santayana employs it, this word, which has recently sunk into a sad misuse, names a special kind of
freedom by which the functioning of the rational intellect
is insulated from the distorting motives which various
creeds and ideologies are continually seeking to impose
upon it. Spinoza was Santayana's prime example of a philosophical mind in which this virtue was realized to an
unsurpassable degree; and as his example indicates, disinterestedness is a virtue that absolutely precludes a philosopher's exercising himself in behalf of transient en-
thusiasms or comforting myths. At bottom, Santayana's
indictment of James and Royce is as severe as it is because
in his view they did not resist the temptation to place
philosophy in the service of a futile anthropomorphism
and its tenacious hope that somehow the world could be
made to reflect back to us an image of our own deepest
moral concerns.

Whether this line of criticism is fair to James and to Royce is another matter. One might concede to Santayana that neither of these thinkers broke as sharply or as decisively with the conception of philosophy as a pillar supporting a moral and a social tradition as he would have wished and yet not find the indictment really convincing. After all, it might be pointed out that Santayana was not nearly as severe in his treatment of the commanding figures of Christian philosophy—an Aquinas or an Augustine—as he was with the far less confident and dogmatic philosophers of a later age who continued to think in moral and teleological terms. Perhaps it was the sheer dogmatic weight of those earlier bodies of doctrine that disposed Santayana more favorably to them than to the hesitant and quizzical speculations of his own colleagues. Perhaps, too, it is not so much the disposition to make human sense of the world process that drew Santayana's fire as it was the failure to carry off this enterprise in the grand style and with full backing of a unitary social authority for the "waking dream" which one thus translates into a rule of life. But beyond that it could be replied to Santayana that the underlying hope that may indeed have motivated much of the philosophical acitivity of a James or a Royce does not give the full measure of the interest of their philosophical achievements. What Santayana's judgment conspicuously fails to do justice to is the fact that these were in their very different ways seminal thinkers. They are still very much worth reading today because, if they raised old questions, they did so in new ways and in ways that draw our attention to features of the matter in hand that bear more thinking about. These are, I submit, "open" philosophies in the sense of that perhaps too much used term which combines both an absence of closure and a vulnerability to revision. In these attributes Santayana could perceive only an irresolute and finally sentimental posture of mind; but definiteness of contour is not the only or necessarily the supreme virtue of a philosophical system or at any rate it should not be if we agree that there is still room for significant inquiry within the domain of philosophy.

It is precisely on this last point that a difficulty arises for Santayana. Suppose that the point of his critique of so much previous philosophy and of the American tradition in particular were to be accepted and all agency and causal efficacy were to be assigned, as he requires, to the realm of matter, what will remain for philosophy to do? More specifically, what legitimate avenues of philosophical self-expression will there be for that interest in the active and moral aspect of human life by which so much philosophical thought has been motivated? Sometimes it almost seems as though the great thesis of naturalism for Santayana was a kind of watershed beyond which no very momentous insights awaited continuing philosophical inquiry; and as already noted, he avoided any involvement in the new movements of philosophical thought, although the fact that their common premise was some form of naturalism might have been expected to make them more congenial to him than their idealistic predecessors were. Interestingly enough, when Santayana called as he did on a number of occasions for the creation of an authentically American philosophy, it appeared that that philosophy should function more as an instrument of national and cultural self-expression than as a deeper apprehension of a common truth. Such a new philosophy—American or otherwise—would apparently have been rather like a new form of poetry in which as in all poetry the circumstances and energies of our natural existence would find their appropriate symbolic equivalents. Although there is little evidence that Santayana found the new continental America more congenial than the

much narrower world of New England, he seemed to feel
that it had a kind of crude vitality which should burst
the hobbles that had been placed upon it by the genteel
tradition and boldly proclaim its vision of itself and of
the world. On the other hand, when a philosophy—that
of John Dewey—did appear on the American scene which
seemed to many to satisfy the criteria laid down by Santayana and which was certainly both emphatically American and aggressively naturalistic, Santayana appraised
it very coolly indeed and imputed to it that same fore-
shortening of moral vision which has the effect of reducing the natural cosmos to the status of a stage pro-
perty for the dramas of human and social existence. In
other words his criticism of Dewey was cast in much the
same terms as those directed against earlier American
systems of thought and also against almost every major
Western philosophy from Plato onward.

What I am trying to bring out with these remarks is
a difficulty which confronts the idea of philosophy as
Santayana appears to conceive it. The essential truth that
a sound philosophy has to communicate is, it seems,
simply that of the dependence of spirit on nature or matter. Unfortunately, philosophy has typically either resisted this truth or has accepted it in a form which subtly
subverts it, as in the case of Dewey's kind of naturalism.
This subversion can take many forms but they all tend to
be characterized by a common disposition to assert some
priority or independence of the ideal elements in human
experience over the natural matrix from which, in Santayana's view, they ultimately derive. A properly conceived naturalistic philosophy, on the other hand, would
give up once and for all the kind of idealistic *hybris* that
runs through the great systematic philosophies from Plato
to Hegel, but when it has done so it will apparently have
exhausted itself. It will survive only in the form of an

aesthetic posture of spirit which has given up any pretentions it may have had to judge or to intervene in the material order on the basis of some requirement, whether moral or otherwise, that derives from its own ideal forms of order. What this conclusion suggests is that Santayana's deepest objection to the moralism which he imputed to the American tradition in philosophy was not so much to the special metaphysical warrant it claimed for itself but rather to its moral character as such, that is, to its willingness to acknowledge a dimension of rationality in which it is truly practical and claims to govern the way we are to act and live.

If there is a difficulty here, and I believe there is, it may be one that relates to the kind of disinterestedness that Santayana imputes to his ideal philosopher. We have already seen that that virtue of disinterestedness precludes any alliance between philosophy and some prevailing social or religious ideology; and it appeared that even if Santayana was less than fair in his actual appreciation of where a Royce or a James stood in relation to the orthodoxies of their time, the standard to which he was holding them was at least a quite unexceptionable one. But a disinterestedness so conceived would certainly not stand in the way of an identification at a deeper level of the interest of philosophy with that of reason understood in its broadest acceptation as the judgmental and critical power. What is problematic and disturbing in Santayana is the fact that his indictment of so many philosophies for what he regards as their willingness to serve as the accomplices of social myth is not really grounded in a stable conception of the deeper interest of philosophy which is thereby betrayed; and because it is not, it tends repeatedly to widen out into a form of disparagement of all philosophies whose espousal of the interest of reason in any way seems to reflect a less omnipresent awareness than Santayana's own of the perilous and conditional status of reason itself within human life. For Santayana rationality as an attribute of human life, whether in its individual or its social form, is a happy accident, the result of a certain balance of natural energies with one another to form a harmonious and satisfying form of life. But just as these moments of harmonious fruition come to pass for reasons that owe little to our wisdom or our capacity, such as it is, to govern our own affairs, so do they pass; and the phase of what Santayana calls rational ethics yields to a postrational phase in which the philosophical mind reconciles itself to its loss by a policy of retrenchment and by surrendering any illusions it may have entertained about the conformity of the way of the world to its own imperious preferences. What Santayana found intolerable and seems to have regarded as a form of incipient madness was any disposition to suppose that the writ of reason, as it may be formulated in some more or less abstract philosophical rendering, runs farther than the ineluctable play of forces in the world of nature in fact permits it to do. A philosophy may be practical in the sense in which many Greek philosophies were, and give an ideal expression to a mode of life that already exists; but if, as is more likely to be the case, the philosopher's relation to human reality is one of conflict, and he nevertheless presumes to raise his voice and insistently addresses imperatives to a refractory world, Santayana quite regularly charges him with having misconceived the relationship of the ideal to the real.

This problem of the authority with which reason can speak, especially in its capacity as practical reason, is a delicate one for all naturalistic philosophies, and for that reason it bears somewhat closer examination. Philosophy may indeed begin with wonder at the vast natural spectacle which confronts us and within which we are ourselves situated; but insofar as philosophy is not simply to be equated with natural science and the systematic development of our knowledge of the processes of nature, it seems to have another kind of origin as well. I would characterize this other origin in terms of an awareness of, and growing interest in, the judgmental and interpretative processes within ourselves which are the necessary mediating term for the apprehensions of natural process in the world at large as well as for the efforts we make to intervene actively in the affairs of nature and of men. Stated in this way, this interest sounds altogether more psychological than it actually has been. In fact, in the case of Plato the interest of which I am speaking took the form of a postulation of a domain of abstract entities quite distinct from both the natural world and from the intellectual soul and its operations; but it seems fair to view this kind of extreme realism as a first approximation, in the material mode, to a theory of the logical or conceptual structure of the knowledge we claim to have of the natural world. In the modern period, it is true, the Platonic two-tiers theory of reality yielded for the most part to an explicitly epistemological and even psychological formulation of the nature of reason; and at the same time this mode of formulation gave rise to a radical scepticism as to the accessibility of a common natural world through the instruments of knowledge that are at our disposal. The problematic status thus assigned to the "external" world stimulated in turn the development of an idealistic theory of mind that emphasized the active functions of mind in the construction of our picture of such a world. More recently still there has been a return to a new version of a nonpsychological theory of knowledge in which language is recognized as the primary medium of conceptualization.

What all these theories have in common is a view of

human consciousness or discourse as the locus of a judgmental activity that is both evaluative and critical in the
sense that it is concerned to fix the content of our beliefs
by means of the shared criteria of validity that apply in
the various domains of thought. There are a number of
different metaphors which can be used for the purpose
of clarifying the distinctive nature of this constitutive
function of human subjectivity and among these one of
the most influential has been the two-substance theory
in which the distinction between this critical-evaluative
function and the world as it emerges from the judgmental
activity through which that function is discharged is
treated as an ontological distinction between two spheres
of being. In the purified or transcendental form of this
essentially Cartesian distinction, however, there is no
longer any attempt to construct a special ontological domicile from which the normative activity described above
would then be thought of as emanating; and the important
point is held to be simply that one not misrepresent that
activity itself by incorporating into one's description of
it all sorts of assumptions about the world itself which,
whatever their merits, cannot claim to render the properly
normative aspect of human subjectivity. Once this point
is understood and with it the irrelevance of attacks upon
it that are really attacks upon the special metaphors that
may have been associated with it, it becomes clear that
there is an intimate connection between philosophy as
such and this transcendental position. This is a position
which we all may be said to occupy just to the extent that
we ask and answer questions about what is the case in the
world; but it is not a position which we are able to con-
ceptualize adequately as long as we remain in the primary
judgmental posture which Husserl referred to as "the
natural attitude." Philosophy is precisely that reflexive
movement of thought in which we become aware of the

distinctive character of the judgmental activity that characterizes that position as well as of the norms to which those judgments appeal. It is in this sense that the interest of philosophy may be said to be identical with that of reason when reason itself is understood as the activity of construing and constituting a world under the governance of a set of shared norms.

If we now bring these observations to bear upon Santayana's conception of reason and the authority it can claim, it turns out that there is a wide area of agreement between the two. There are indeed, as Santayana so often reminds us, a thousand natural conditions that must be satisfied before the power of rational judgment can be effectively realized within human life. Many of these are still unknown to us and, even if known, might still elude any effective control over them. It is also true, as we know to our sorrow, that at least as many circumstances seem to conspire against the achievement of that collective form of rationality that we hope may one day characterize the actions of human societies. In short, the situation and prospects of human rationality remain, for all the great triumphs it has made possible, just as precarious and vulnerable as Santayana declares them to be. And yet these facts need not be taken as being quite so prejudicial to the wider authority of reason as Santayana seems to assume. For one thing, however dependent the operation of our rational faculties may be on the accidents of our physical constitution, it does not follow that the internal form of their rationality—its characteristic normative structure—is simply a transcription of some feature of the natural order, or that a knowledge of our physical constitution would put us in a position to say what the structure of our rational processes must be. However often philosophers may celebrate the end of the various bifurcations of nature, they have yet to show how this one can be overcome, and in fact it still serves to delimit the area in which they themselves work. Beyond this internal kind of autonomy which can be claimed for reason, there is another respect in which it may be said to govern our perspective even on the very events by which it is so often overcome. By that I mean that once reason has appeared in the world, those who understand its authority at all owe an unconditional allegiance to the possibility of life it represents; and what this means in practice is that they must view and judge the course of the world from the standpoint of the interest of reason. If philosophers are precisely those human beings to whom the authority of reason should be most evident simply by virtue of the way their own special focus of interest is defined, then surely it must follow that a philosopher may never be indifferent or cynical in his sponsorship of the claims of reason, even when these enjoy little or no respect in the world at large. He cannot celebrate vitality simply because it is vitality and he cannot as it were jump over to the side of "life" or "spontaneity" when to do so means turning a deaf ear to the claims of reason. This is not because life and spontaneity are bad things, but because they cannot replace and must finally themselves remain subject to a judgment whose normative status rests on grounds other then mere impulse or force.

With these observations we have reached a point at which the distinctive and (to me) unacceptable feature of a naturalism like Santayana's may be clearly perceived. Santayana, who did not like Hegel, used to say that he (Hegel) was rather like a spectator at a cockfight who would cheer on both contenders with equal enthusiasm because the important thing was not that either should win but rather that the contest itself should be as intense and passionate as possible, presumably for the sake of some supervening benefit that would quite transcend the subjective purposes of the participants. But if Hegel's kind of impartiality seems cold-blooded and finally repellent, as Santayana manifestly wants us to conclude, it was at least connnected with a conception, however fanciful it may seem, of a teleological ordering of human history within which an intelligible ideal was thought to be moving toward realization. By contrast, the standpoint which Santayana adopted and from which he viewed the events of the human as well as of the natural world was that of "nature"—that is, of a world process that was neither moral nor teleological nor rational in any sense other than that of its putative regularity and upon which the human forms or order which these adjectives denote have been all too incautiously projected. The question this raises is quite simply what it can mean to adopt such a standpoint for the purpose of reviewing and criticizing what Santayana himself calls "the life of reason." This is really to ask whether it is possible for philosophy which has been so closely identified with an interest in the internal ordering structures of that life to stand, as it were, outside it and to interpret it in the light of its shifting relationship to its natural milieu. The question is a momentous one in connection with any general appraisal of Santayana's philosophical achievement since the undertaking so described is the one he set himself in the work which bears the name of *The Life of Reason* and which most students of Santayana still regard as his most substantial achievement. Accordingly, the remainder of this paper will be devoted to a discussion of that work and, in particular, of the naturalistic standpoint from which it is written.

II.

It is important to begin this discussion by taking note of the way the conception of *The Life of Reason* took shape in Santayana's mind. In the preface he added in 1922, he tells us that "the first suggestion for such a work had come to me in my student days, on reading Hegel's *Phä-nomenologie des Geistes*"; and he goes on to say that in that work "a very fine subject . . . the history of human ideas" has been spoiled by the sophistry implicit in Hegel's own conception of his work.[2] Hegel's ambition, according to Santayana, was "to show that the episodes he happened to review formed a dialectical chain . . . and that this history of human ideas made up the whole of cosmic evolution." "It occurred to me," Santayana continues, "that a more honest criticism of progress might be based on tracing the distracted efforts of man to satisfy his impulses in his natural environment."[3] In this same preface Santayana also acknowledges that he may not have been altogether faithful to this conception of the work which sets it in such sharp opposition to the Hegelian program of standing wholly within the life of the mind and showing how its successive forms are generated by a logic that is completely independent of the impulses and needs imposed by our natural situation. Possibly, Santayana suggests, he may have slipped into the subjectivistic posture too often and thus elided, for example, the all-important distinction between nature and the idea of nature; but the intention of the work was nevertheless to display the life of reason as unfolding within a natural setting that was quite emphatically not of its own devising and as responding in its various ways to the insistent requirements which a necessitous animal must constantly satisfy. Interestingly enough, Santayana contrasts the normative character of his own review of the "phases of human progress" with Hegel's alleged neutrality, and he declares that he "could not write the life of reason without distinguishing it from madness."[4] This madness turns out to consist of a tendency to suppose that "nothing but human discourse can exist or that nature must be composed of the rhetorical unities of familiar discourse."[5] It is, we are told, "important that human discourse should acknowledge the far deeper embosoming realms of matter and of essence" and in *The Life of Reason* it was "the murmur of nature in human discourse that was called reason and that the author attempted to catch and interpret."

A naturalistic phenomenology of mind as Santayana conceived it is certainly an ambitious undertaking—almost as ambitious in its way as Hegel's own and not really less susceptible to very serious challenge. But the original impulse to the creation of such a work is without question an attractive one. Whether or not we accept Santayana's characterization of the idealistic aberrations that in his view transform the *Phenomenology of Mind* finally into "myth and sophistry," there can be no doubt that in its inner logic that work functions rather like a vacuum cleaner that sucks up into itself everything with which it comes into contact. Against that tendency of the kind of philosophy that begins in empiricism and ends in idealism, Santayana repeatedly argues in an essentially simple but powerful way that we must distinguish between, on the one hand, the meaning that the mind entertains and that serves as a necessary enabling condition for our apprehending an object of the kind it denotes and, on the other, that object itself. When these two are confused and when meanings or concepts are thought of as operating within the sphere of thought or experience or mind, then necessarily the objects that have been inextricably tied to these meanings are similarly pulled into the orbit of that same experience; and we are left without a way of expressing the representative or self-transcending character of knowledge. But once we free ourselves from these perverted psychological assumptions and understand what we should never have forgotten, namely, that to know something is not to absorb or consume it, we are also liberated from the prejudice which precludes our speaking of human thought and experience as though they had no natural domicile. The very same knowledge of the natural environment that is the product of our various conceptualizations of experience can be utilized for the purpose of helping us to identify the forces that form intelligence and to which it in turn is variously responsive. Santayana's sometimes rather exaggerated preference for the philosophical ethos of the ancients over that of the moderns is due in large part to the fact that the former never entered the epistemological blind alleys of a Hume or a Kant and were therefore able to construct a theory of human reason that could do justice to both its finite and conditioned character and its normative authority without any of the hypocritical skepticism that Santayana imputed to Kant or the cosmic egotism of his followers.

All of this, one feels, is very soundly conceived and at the time a much needed antidote to the highfalutin philosophies of *Geist* and its wondrous works. And yet it remains unclear just how far Santayana thinks the legitimation of nature as the domicile of reason will take him and how much of his natural history of mind can really be be gathered from natural sources. One thing is certain, and that is that Santayana was never really a materialist in the strong ontological sense which would require a physicalistic definition of consciousness. Spirit—Santayana's term for consciousness as such—is irreducible to the realm of matter although it is compelled to abandon its claim to causal efficacy to the latter and survives the wreck of its effort to spin its own dialectical patterns into the operations of the physical world only in the form of a pure contemplative activity. In this connection it is interesting to note the distinctly haughty distaste Santayana expresses for the speculations of the younger American realists who under the influence of William James were attempting to deny any distinctive ontological status to consciousness—an attempt which Santayana sees as the boomerang effect of the earlier idealism which identified things with ideas and now was compelled to see this equation turned against it in the form of the assertion that ideas are things. Here—more perhaps than anywhere else—one senses that something very dear to Santayana is being put in danger and that something is the imaginative life and the special freedom that accrues to spirit when it gives up its misguided attempt to rule the world or even human affairs and gives itself over to the impartial enjoyment of the infinite realm of essence. But this defense of imagination as the one domain in which spirit is not controlled by nature only because it in turn makes no effort to exercise any reciprocating control conceals a hidden premise. That premise takes the form of an identification of the realm of truth—the compendium of true propositions concerning what occurs in the world—with the truths of science and an exclusion of considerations of purpose and value from the executive order of events in the world. What this means in practice is that as a philosopher of human culture Santayana is committed to a fundamentally dichotomous approach to the several domains of distinctively human activity, such as, for example, art, religion, and morality. The terms of the dichotomy are the efficacious order of events in the realm of matter and the imaginative elaboration or symbolization which these receive at the level of human consciousness; and Santayana's claim must be that the latter is a kind of coded transcription of the former in which, as he so often puts it, moral and dramatic unities symbolize, however imperfectly, real causal connections. What all this implies of course is that there is no prospect of our being able to defend the autonomy of these nonscientific symbolic forms on the ground that they contribute to our understanding of any real event or situation, but only on the ground that they represent an enrichment of the imaginative life. Santayana was fond of quoting Goethe's line, *"Am farbigen Abglanz haben wir das Leben,"* and it is at bottom the color and variety that art or religion add to our lives that must in his view justify them.

If with these observations in mind one turns to the actual discussions of the several domains of human culture in *The Life of Reason,* it turns out that Santayana is not really at great pains to show in detail how that upward translation of natural forces into their symbolic representations actually takes place, much less to put the general thesis that formulates this relationship to an empirical test against the materials available from these domains. The naturalistic thesis in the form that has already been indicated is simply assumed as a premise and then an account is given, whether of "society" or "religion" or "art," in which strong emphasis is placed on the expressive function of a given mode of thought, that is, on the multiple ways in which it presupposes the natural situation of human beings as the naturalistic philosopher perceives it. Since there are, on almost any reasonable interpretation, innumerable respects in which our structures of belief bear the mark of our natural situation and of the multiple needs and interests it inspires, it is hardly surprising that such accounts should, in the hands of as skillful an interpreter as Santayana, achieve a real plausibility. And yet there is something curiously disappointing about the procedure that Santayana follows in his exploration of one area of human culture after another. Although he has often been described, in contrast to many other prosaic philosophers, as having great powers of sympathetic divination for forms of meaning and intent that are alien to or remote from our everyday experience, the procedure he follows is often not very different from that of an historian in the period of the Enlightenment when confronted by a piece of doctrine or social practice that he could not possibly square with his own fundamental beliefs. The reflex of such a mind is typically to describe the phenomenon in privative terms as a lack or absence of the qualities of mind which by his own standard are the ones that would be genuinely appropriate to the situation under consideration. In Santayana's philosophical lexicon the two valid categories that are used again and again for sorting out some otherwise anomalous phenomenon are imagination and physics. The one addresses itself to the ideal and can symbolize, but never control, the actual course of events. The other, which human beings have been able to utilize only in its most primitive common-sense form during most of their history, explains why things happen as they do and has nothing to do with their ideal values. But even if one were to subscribe to Santayana's way of interpreting this contrast, it would still be an open question whether one can really get at the most characteristic features of some major symbolic form by means of an analysis cast in terms of such a contrast as this.

In this connection Santayana's treatment of religion may serve as a case in point. It has often been regarded as perhaps the most successful demonstration of his powers of intuitive understanding; and it is certainly the case that here, if anywhere, his initial naturalistic premise will be widely endorsed, since many are likely to agree with Santayana in thinking that what we now call "religious discourse" finally lacks a referent. But this initial judgment relieves us of the obligation—surely incumbent upon a philosopher of culture—to inquire into the internal structure of mythic and religious thought as well as such inner potentialities for development as it may hold within itself. If Santayana is right and at a certain stage of human enlightenment "religion" finally was understood to have only one valid ingredient—that of moral imagination— which had been improperly associated with a chimerical cosmology, it still does not follow that it is properly described as having consisted from its inception in a mixture of moralized cosmology with externalized poetry. Again, to argue as Santayana does, that religion—illusion that it is—owes its existence to the fact that man "is afraid of a universe that leaves him alone" and "cannot respect an ideal that is not imposed on him against his will" seems to be perilously close to arguing in a circle.[6] Such an argument imputes to man a capacity for being disturbed by the possible nonexistence of God and derives from that his belief in a deity when it is precisely the capacity for conceiving this kind of absence—a capacity which no other animal appears to have—that is as much in need of explanation as is the positive belief itself. Whether there are naturalistic explanations for the emergence of the forms of thought we call religious is not a matter that can be settled a priori, but one does feel that Santayana has underestimated the kind of jump beyond animal experi- ence that the postulation of gods involves and that he has done less than justice to religion as a medium of thought. Surely, one feels, whether or not monotheism appealed to the desire of the Jews not to allow other people to have gods, it represents something far more significant in the intellectual history of mankind than such an imputation of motives can possibly convey.

The case of religion suggests that, while the points of contact between a symbolic form and our experience of the natural world may be numerous and important, that fact does not suffice to justify a treatment of that form or mode of thought as though it were simply a transcription of a natural situation. Nevertheless, Santayana's analysis of religion is likely to maintain its appeal if only because of a deep-seated and widely shared feeling that religious discourse generates no acceptable canon of truth, no matter what internal complexity and distinctiveness it may achieve, and that as a result its only significance *must* be the expressive relationship in which it stands to our natural being. It may be useful, therefore, to examine Santayana's treatment of morality rather than religion since the claim of the former to a permanent place within the spectrum of the forms of human thought can be plausibly regarded as being stronger than those of religion. Certainly the strategy of argument that Santayana uses in dealing with morality is generally very similar to the one already noted in connection with his treatment of religion. That strategy is to concentrate attention at the outset on the many natural conditions that are presupposed by any ordering of individual or social life that is at all likely to satisfy the criteria of what Santayana calls "rational ethics": the existence of actual needs and interests in assignable individual persons; the power that is needed to protect these interests and the ordering they assume from destructive interference by alien agencies; the level of culture and the temper of mind that are the enabling conditions for a shared discourse directed toward the harmonization of many distinct wills. All of this natural substructure of the moral life is very convincingly sketched in by Santayana. Indeed the account is so skillfully presented that one can easily miss the fact that this preparatory groundwork for rational ethics also constitutes virtually the whole of what Santayana has to say on the subject. Concerning the ideal or rule or principle that is to govern our actions and by reference to which the moral quality of those actions would be determined, Santayana can really say only that it is a "force energising in the

world, discovering its affinities there and clinging to them
to the exclusion of their hateful opposites" . . . "an ideal
embodying the particular demands, possibilities, and satisfactions of a specific being."[7] "The direct aim of reason
is harmony,"[8] we are told, and "the true conscience is . . .
an integrated natural will, chastened by a clear knowledge
of what it pursues and may attain."[9] With these presuppositions, it is not surprising to learn that "sympathy and
justice are simply an expansion of the soul's interests,
arising when we consider other men's lives so intently
that something in us imitates and re-enacts their experience, so that we move partly in unison with their movement, recognise the reality and initial legitimacy of their
interests and consequently regard their aims in our action,
insofar as our own status and purposes have become identical with theirs."[10]

Nowhere in this discussion is there any hint that the
principle of justice might imply a constraint on action
to which "nature" by virtue of one of those happy but
unstable harmonies which she effects has not already given
an implicit consent. Rational morality, it seems, can come
into being only when nature has antecedently done her
work and this work comprehends not only the creation of
the conditions which make it possible for practical reasons
to exercise its ordering function at all, but also the natural
sympathies and affinities which reason will then recognize and codify. This conception of morality is associated
by Santayana with the names of Socrates and Aristotle,
and it is a eudaimonistic ethic in the sense that duty and
obligation enjoy no status that is not instrumental to some
ideal of well-being. But the "nature" of Aristotle is not
at all the same thing as the "nature" of Santayana; and if
it does not generate directives which run counter to inclination with the remorseless severity of a Kant, they
certainly seem to have a stronger measure of normative

authority than do the ratifications of the actual to which reason perforce must confine itself under Santayana's naturalistic dispensation. What is perhaps most remarkable about the latter's way of conceiving the province of morality is the fact that it emphasizes so strongly the role of the ideal and yet this ideal turns out not to incorporate in any very prominent way what one might have thought would constitute its chief claim to being described as ideal. I have in mind here the formal constraints by which the common validity of some maxim of action for an open class of rational agents has traditionally been expressed. But if reason in its practical aspect can never impose a discipline that extends farther than do the energies and affinities of the "particular life" in which it is grounded and if all duty is at bottom "a matter of self-knowledge" and thus an amplification rather than a restriction of "a living and particular will," we might be tempted to conclude that this conception is much closer to Hume's doctrine of a reason than "is, and ought only to be the slave of the passions" than it is to the moral philosophy of the ancient world with which Santayana associates it.

Brief as they are, these observations on Santayana's treatment of morality may give support to some of the doubts that were expressed earlier about the capacity of a naturalistic philosophy—a philosophy which like Santayana's assumes the standpoint of nature for the purpose of giving an account of the life of reason—to do justice to the distinctive nature and requirements of the order which reason seeks to introduce. It is the great merit of such philosophies to draw our attention to the multiple ways in which the ideals that preside over the moral life are rooted in the practical necessities of material existence and of social life. At the same time they appear to lack a means of recognizing the fact that these same elements of reason that are at work in the primary coordination of human wills that makes it possible for a society to exist at all, are also susceptible of an ideal extension and generalization in the course of which their abstract rational form is first exhibited. It was the error of rationalism to argue that these abstract models of rationality express the essential nature of man or of society and thus to ground their authority on an ontological claim. But it is surely an even more serious error to suppose, as the naturalistic philosopher does, that the authority that can be claimed by a principle of, say, rational morality can run no farther than the natural forces by which it may be in fact supported. A more satisfactory approach to all these matters might be one that enables us to acknowledge that in the domain of morality as in other domains of human culture the rationality we deploy as the instrument of our natural interests and needs has a way of asserting its authority even over those who would allow it only the status of an instrument and that it draws us on into a realm of implication that may be remote indeed from the interests which we had hoped to make reason serve. This peculiarly ambiguous nature of reason, setting itself up as master in the house of nature where it has been admitted only through a fortuitous conjunction of circumstances and where it remains subject to peremptory and sudden ejection, seems to me to be just the aspect that neither rationalism nor naturalism succeeds in capturing. Rationalism insists on the validity of this claim to authority and gives scant attention to the degree of congruence between that claim and such natural dispositions as may be available to give it effect. Naturalism, in contrast, seems to be wholly intent on the kind of footing reason can secure in its natural terrain and observes—not without satisfaction—that when reason tries to do without that kind of support it promptly comes crashing down to earth again. It seems obvious that the idea of philosophy as a principled espousal of the interest of reason stands to suffer from both of these strategies—in the one case, through a premature absolutization, and in the other, by being put on far too short a leash. Santayana was remarkably sensitive to the kind of distortion of the role of reason that results from the first of these, and his critique of the main tradition of American philosophy reflects a justified dissatisfaction with its tendency to secure the imperatives of reason too completely against the accidents of its natural habitat. What this paper has attempted to show is that the naturalistic alternative he offered was not really a very much more satisfactory one. Perhaps it has also succeeded in showing how, in spite of all his express disassociation of his thought from the concerns of most other twentieth-century philosophers, it nevertheless exhibits many of the same conflicts by which naturalism in its present-day version has yet to resolve.

Footnotes

1. George Santayana, *Character and Opinion in America* (New York, W. W. Norton and Co., 1967).
2. George Santayana, *Reason in Common Sense*, Vol. I of *The Life of Reason* (New York, Collier Books, 1962), 10.
3. *Ibid.*
4. *Ibid.*
5. *Ibid.*, 11.
6. Santayana, *Reason in Religion*, Vol. III of *The Life of Reason*, 68.
7. *Ibid.*, 174.
8. *Ibid.*, 178.
9. *Ibid.*, 183.
10. *Ibid.*, 175.

Facts of the Matter

W. V. Quine

It was emphasized by rationalists and empiricists alike that inquiry should begin with clear ideas. I agree about the clarity, but I balk at ideas. The British empiricists themselves balked at abstract ideas. *Nihil in mente*, they declared in their orotund British measures, *quod non prius in sensu*. They echoed their nominalist ancestors, for whom abstract ideas were *flatus vocis*—words, words, words.

What then about concrete ideas? Even a strictly sensory idea is elusive unless it is reinforced by language. This point was made by Wittgenstein. Unaided by language, we might treat a great lot of sensory events as recurrences of one and the same sensation, simply because of a similarity between each and the next; and yet there can have been a serious cumulative slippage of similarity between the latest of these events and the earliest of them. But if we have learned society's word for the sensation, then social intercourse will arrest the drift and keep us in line. We will be saved by the statistical fact that the speakers have not all drifted in the same direction.

Let us therefore recognize that the whole idea idea, abstract and concrete, is a frail reed indeed. We must seek a firm footing rather in words. The point was urged by John Horne Tooke only shortly after Hume's time, in 1786. Tooke held that Locke's essay could be much improved by substituting the word 'word' everywhere for the word 'idea'. What is thereby gained in firmness is attended by no appreciable loss in scope, since ideas without words would have come to little in any event. We think mostly in words, and we report our thoughts wholly in words. Let us then take one leaf from the old-time philosophy and another from John Horne Tooke. Philosophical inquiry should begin with the clear, yes; but with clear words.

And what words are those? It will not do to say that they are the words that express clear ideas, or the words that clearly express ideas, for we are fleeing the idea idea. For a standard of clarity of language we must look rather to the social character of language and the use of language in communication. Bypassing the idea idea, we can still do something with clarity of communication. The vehicle of communication is the sentence, and one mark of clarity of communication is agreement as to the truth of the sentence. This is a very fallible criterion, but it is a beginning. Let us see what we can do to improve it.

If one party affirms a sentence and the other party assents, this gives little evidence of communication; for a purely random verdict would be affirmative half the time. However, there is some safety in numbers. Instead of relativizing our clarity criterion to two communicants, we may relativize it to increasing sectors of the speech community. We might consider what proportion of the community would be prepared to agree to the truth or falsity of a sentence, and we might take this figure as a measure of the clarity of the sentence.

This is better, but it still will not do. One difficulty is that there are cults, fads, and slogans that can sweep a community, prompting widespread agreement to the truth of sentences that a clear thinker would not rate as clear in the slightest. Another and opposite difficulty is that people can disagree regarding the truth of a sentence even when the sentence would be said to be clear. Now both of these difficulties can be met by appealing once

again to numbers: by appealing to what Mill called con-
comitant variation.

For this purpose we direct our attention to a special sort
of sentences, *occasion* sentences. These are the sentences
that admit of verdicts and truth values not once for all
but from one occasion of utterance to another, depending
on what is going on in the neighborhood. They are sentences like 'It's raining', 'This is red', 'That's his uncle',
'He owes me money', 'There goes a rabbit'. Historical
truths are not among them, nor are scientific hypotheses,
nor credos, nor slogans. Now we might measure the clarity
of an occasion sentence by the readiness of witnesses to
agree in their verdicts on it from occasion to occasion. By
this standard 'It's raining' and 'This is red' rate high;
'There goes a rabbit' not quite so high; 'That's his uncle'
rates lower; 'He owes me money' lower still. There are
three possible responses—assent, dissent, and abstention—
and we may also distinguish degrees of hesitation. The
great value of this standard of clarity lies in its linking of
language to nonlinguistic reality.

The occasion sentences that pass this clarity test with
high marks are what I call observation sentences. They
often take the form simply of single nouns or adjectives—
'Rabbit', 'Raining'—but for our purposes they are best
thought of still as sentences, admitting of assent or dissent
in the light of each present local situation. They are
expressions that we have learned to associate with publicly
observable concurrent circumstances. Previous speakers
have taught us some of these expressions by direct conditioning to the circumstances. They are circumstances
which, thanks to their public character, can be appreciated
jointly by us and our teachers. Some of these observational
expressions also are learned indirectly by some of us,
through explanations in other words; but all could be
learned in the direct way, such is their observational

character. They are our introduction to language, for they are the expressions that we can learn to use without learning to use others first. It is through them that language and science imbibe their empirical content. It is back to or toward them, also, that a scientist reverts when he is mustering evidence for a disputed hypothesis; for the distinctive trait of an observation sentence is that present witnesses will usually agree about it on the spot.

Earlier I made Wittgenstein's point: how public language anchors experience, arresting drift. Now we are noting the converse: how public experience anchors language. The observation sentence is the anchor line.

I remarked that the use of an observation sentence often is and always could be acquired directly by conditioning. This process is also called induction. By either name it is the learning process at its simplest. If an event resembles an earlier one, the subject tends to expect its sequel to resemble the sequel of the earlier one. The expectation hinges thus on similarity in some sense—similarity by the subject's own lights. This relation is one of subjective similarity, and no significance need be sought for it apart from the consequent inductive expectations themselves. From a behavioral point of view a subject's expectations are shown by his overt behavior, and his similarity standards are shown by the pattern of his expectations.

Expectations are in large part fulfilled, despite the subjectivity of similarity standards; ours is a fairly friendly world. Evolutionary biology explains this by the fact that those standards are largely innate and thus favored by natural selection according to their survival value.

Primitive inductive learning is evident in the acquisition of various observation sentences. To acquire an observation sentence is to learn when to expect a veteran speaker to approve one's utterance of it, or to assent to it on his own account. This can be learned from sample instances by induction: by extrapolating to further cases along lines of subjective similarity. These linguistic inductions tend to be highly successful — more so still than the general run of inductions in our fairly friendly world. The reason is that whereas one's inductions regarding nature owe their success only to a rough congruity between one's similarity standards and the trend of events in nature, on the other hand one's inductions regarding the veteran speaker's assent to the observation sentence owe their success to a sharing of similarity standards by the speaker and oneself. Heredity, environment, and social interaction have fostered such sharing of similarity standards to a high degree.

Direct conditioning or simple induction does not suffice for the acquisition of language generally. The learning process has to be more elaborate when we move on to grammatical constructions, to past and future tenses, to conditionals and conjecturals and metaphors, and to theoretical and abstract terms. It is evident that these further linguistic structures are based, however precariously, on the observational vocabulary that was learned by direct confrontation and simple conditioning. The superstructure is cantilevered outward from that foundation by imitation and analogy, by trial and error. In the course of mastering it we may check up now and again by noting the reaction of the listener. But it is in the observational vocabulary that language makes its principal contact with experience. It is this part of language that we first learn to apply, and to which we retreat when a check point is needed.

The situations that command assent to a given observation sentence will not be quite alike. They will be similar by our lights and by the lights of other speakers. But we can count on a curious tolerance of spatial reorientation in these similarity standards. We can see why if we reflect that the language learner and his informant are not situated eye to eye. They see things from unlike angles, receiving somewhat unlike presentations. The learner is thus made to associate with his presentation a word or occasion sentence that was elicited from the informant by a somewhat different presentation. It will have to be a versatile word or sentence indifferently applicable throughout a whole group of presentations.

My talking of observation sentences rather than observation terms is a matter of first things first. We can learn to assent to and dissent from observation sentences as wholes, under appropriate stimulatory conditions, with no thought of what sentences or parts of sentences to count as terms or what objects to count them as referring to. And now what happens when at last we can be said to use some of these sentences or parts of sentences as terms denoting some sort of supposed objects?

The main thing to settle, in the way of fixing the objects, is their individuation: we have to fix standards of sameness and difference. Now it is clear that at this point little or no attention will be paid to differences of perspective; for we saw that such differences are bound to be transcended in the learning of words. What are posited as objects for the terms to refer to will be, primarily, objects that are counted identical under changes of perspective. This explains the primacy of bodies. If clarity can be ascribed to things as well as to words, then bodies are things at their clearest. If inquiry is to begin with what is clear, then let us begin as physicalists.

The move from sentences to terms is already a major step in language learning. On the one hand there is the simple observation sentence 'Rabbit', comparable to 'Red' or 'It's raining'; it commands assent in the presence of rabbits. On the other hand there is the term 'rabbit', which denotes the rabbits. A speaker may be said to have mastered this term, and to have achieved objective reference, only when he has learned to subject the term to all the grammatical apparatus of particles and constructions that go to implement objective reference: the apparatus of singular and plural, of definite and indefinite articles, of pronominal cross reference, of identity and distinctness, and of counting. When he has come this far he has risen above the primitive base afforded by observation sentences, and has ventured somewhat out onto the cantilevered superstructure. Language learning at this stage is beyond the reach of simple induction; it proceeds by imitation and analogy in more complicated ways.[1]

Various of the one-word observation sentences like 'Rabbit' and 'Apple', which were themselves learned in the simple inductive way, will now spawn terms in their likeness—terms denoting bodies. The terms are already theoretical. A body is conceived as retaining its identity over time between appearances. Whether we encounter the same body the next time around, the same apple, for instance, or only another one like it, is a question not to be settled by simple induction. It is settled, if at all, by inference from a network of hypotheses that we have internalized littly by little in the course of acquiring the nonobservational superstructure of our language. These hypotheses are supported only indirectly by past observation: they owe their plausibility to our having inferred other consequences from them that were borne out by observation. Such is the continuing method of science: not simple induction, but the hypothetico-deductive method.

Bodies are basic to our way of thought, as objects go. They are the paradigmatic objects, clearer and more perspicuous than others. Imitation and analogy continue their work, however, not stopping with an ontology of bodies. Grammatical analogy between general terms and singular terms encourages us to treat a general term as if it designated a single object, and thus we come to posit a realm of objects for the general terms to designate: a realm of properties, or sets. What with the nominalizing also of verbs and clauses, a vaguely varied and very untidy ontology grows up.

The common man's ontology is vague and untidy in two ways. It takes in many purported objects that are vaguely or inadequately defined. But also, what is more significant, it is vague in its scope; we cannot even tell in general which of these vague things to ascribe to a man's ontology at all, which things to count him as assuming. Should we regard grammar as decisive? Does every noun demand some array of denotata? Surely not; the nominalizing of verbs is often a mere stylistic variation. But where can we draw the line?

It is a wrong question; there is no line to draw. Bodies are assumed, yes; they are the things, first and foremost. Beyond them there is a succession of dwindling analogies. Various expressions come to be used in ways more or less parallel to the use of the terms for bodies, and it is felt that corresponding objects are more or less posited, *pari passu*; but there is no purpose in trying to mark an ontological limit to the dwindling parallelism.

It is only our somewhat regimented and sophisticated language of science that has evolved in such a way as really to raise ontological questions. It is an object-oriented idiom. Any idiom purports to tell the truth, but this idiom purports, more specifically, to tell about objects. Its referential apparatus, the apparatus for referring to objects, is explicit; there is no question of a dwindling parallelism. Just what those objects are—what else besides bodies—is still as may be; but it becomes a significant question, and it can be variously answered in various scientific systems of the world.

The basic structure of the language of science has been isolated and schematized in a familiar form. It is the predicate calculus: the logic of quantification and truth functions. In representing it thus I do not mean to take issue with those quantum physicists who recommend a different logic of a non-truth-functional kind, but I set them aside in order not to complicate the picture. Also I do not mean to deprecate alternative formulations of standard logic, such as predicate-functor logic; but as long as these are intertranslatable with the classical predicate calculus, we lose nothing in adhering to the latter. For concreteness, then, let us adhere to it; for it is familiar.

Language thus regimented has a simple grammar. There is a lexicon of predicates. Each atomic sentence of the language consists of a predicate, say an n-place predicate, adjoined to n variables. The rest of the sentences are built up of the atomic ones by truth functions and quantification.

Thus the only singular terms are the variables, used for quantification. It would be all right to allow also names as further singular terms and to allow functors for building complex singular terms from the names and the variables. But we can pass over these further conveniences; for there are well-known ways of dispensing with them, however inconveniently, by systematic paraphrasing of contexts.

When language is thus regimented, its ontology comprises just the objects that the variables of quantification admit as values. Some of the turns of phrase in ordinary language that seem to involve novel sorts of objects will disappear under the regimentation. Still we must not expect to end up with bodies as the only values of the variables. Much of the positing of abstract objects that seems to go on in ordinary language proves to be gratuitous and eliminable, but much of it also proves valuable. How *sets* can pay their way is classically illustrated by the definition of the *closed iterate* of a two-place predicate. Ancestor, for instance, is the closed iterate of parent. Neither parenthood nor ancestry has to do with sets, but sets enable us to define ancestor in terms of parent. For every predicate in our language we can express also its closed iterate, if we allow ourselves to quantify over sets as values of our variables.

It must be emphasized that when we reckon the ontology as comprising just the values of the variables, we are assuming the strictly regimented notation: just predicates, variables, quantifiers, and truth functions. Admission of additional linguistic elements can upset this ontological standard. Thus suppose someone adopts outright an operator for forming the closed iterates of predicates, instead of defining it with help of an ontology of sets. Are we to say that he has saved on ontology? I say rather that he has shelved the ontological question by switching to a language that is not explicit on ontology. His ontology is indeterminate, except relative to some agreed translation of his notation into our regimented one.

Another way in which quantification over sets or numbers or other abstract objects can sometimes be avoided is by admitting a modal operator of necessity,[2] if we can see our way to making appropriate sense of this device. Here again we are presented not with an ontological saving, but with a question of foreign exchange.

We have just been seeing how the values of the variables may understate the ontology in the presence of some foreign notations. Other foreign notations may work oppositely. If idioms of propositional attitude were admitted, such as 'x believes that p', then the variables might seem to overreach the ontology; for x can believe that $(\exists y)$ (y is a unicorn) without there being any unicorns. The ontological question for such a language, as for ordinary language generally, makes sense only relative to agreed translations into ontologically regimented notation. A language is not necessarily defective in being thus ontologically indecisive; it is just not a language of the object-oriented type.

Translation of ordinary language into the regimented idiom is not determinate. For some sentences there are various acceptable regimentations not equivalent to one another in point of ontology, and for some sentences there is no acceptable regimentation at all. In general this translation venture is significant only when undertaken systematically for a substantial corpus of sentences, a branch of science, rather than for stray sentences in isolation. Many sentences that seem from their grammatical form to talk of abstract objects of various sorts will be translated into regimented sentences that are innocent of those ontic commitments, for the translator will favor ontic economy where he can. Regiment as he will, however, he cannot make do with just bodies. By quantifying over classes he increases the yield of his apparatus, as illustrated by the closed iterates. By quantifying over numbers and functions he is able to make systematic use of measurement and thus to develop his scientific theory along quantitative lines.

These sets, numbers, and functions are posited, as denizens of the universe supplementary to the primordial bodies, in order to strengthen and simplify the overall theory. To do so is not to repudiate physicalism. The physicalist does not insist on an exclusively corporeal ontology. He is content to declare bodies to be *fundamental* to nature in somewhat this sense: there is no difference *in the world* without a difference in the positions or states of bodies. I say 'in the world' so as not to include differences between abstract objects, as of mathematics.

My qualification 'in the world' may seem to deprive the

statement of content, as if to say that there is no difference in the *physical* world without a difference in the positions or states of bodies. I may better phrase the matter in terms of *change*: there is no change without a change in the positions or states of bodies. This serves still to exempt mathematical objects, which are changeless.

One application of this physicalist principle is to dispositions. There is no change even in unactualized dispositions without physical change, no difference in dispositions without physical difference. But the main thrust of the doctrine, of course, is its bearing on mental life. If a man were twice in the same physical state, then, the physicalist holds, he would believe the same things both times, he would have the same thoughts, and he would have all the same unactualized dispositions to thought and action. Where positions and states of bodies do not matter, there is no fact of the matter.

It is not a reductionist doctrine of the sort sometimes imagined. It is not a utopian dream of our being able to specify all mental events in physiological or microbiological terms. It is not a claim that such correlations even exist, in general, to be discovered; the groupings of events in mentalistic terms need not stand in any systematic relation to biological groupings.[3] What it does say about the life of the mind is that there is no mental difference without a physical difference. Most of us nowadays are so ready to agree to this principle that we fail to sense its magnitude. It is a way of saying that the fundamental objects are the physical objects. It accords physics its rightful place as the basic natural science without venturing any dubious hopes of reduction of other disciplines. It has further important implications that we tend not to see.

If there is no mental difference without a physical difference, then there is pointless ontological extravagance in admitting minds as entities over and above bodies; we lose nothing by applying mentalistic predicates directly to persons as bodies, much in the manner of everyday usage. We still have two species of predicates, mental and physical, but both sorts apply to bodies. Thus it is that the physicalist comes out with an ontology of just physical objects, together with the sets or other abstract objects of mathematics; no minds as additional entities.

Note that the situation is not symmetrical. The converse move of dispensing with bodies in favor of minds is not open to us, for we would not allow that there is no physical difference in the world without a mental difference—not unless we were idealists.

I have been talking easily of physical predicates, physical differences, as over against mental ones. Until this notion is better defined or delimited, my formulations of physicalism are inadequate. Thus take the dictum 'no mental difference without a physical difference'. We must not explain 'physical difference' merely as any difference between bodies; this would trivialize the dictum. For, even if we were to recognize minds as entities distinct from bodies and merely associated with them, it would be trivial to say that there is no difference in states of mind without a difference in the associated bodies. The bodies differ at least to the extent of being associated with minds that are in those different states.

Thus the dictum tells us nothing until we define 'physical difference' more narrowly. Similarly for my preceding versions of physicalism: 'no difference in the world without a difference in the positions or states of bodies', 'no change without a change in the positions or states of bodies'. We must say what to count as states of bodies.

One major motivation of physics down the centuries might be said to have been just that: to say what counts as a physical difference, a physical trait, a physical state. The question can be put more explicitly thus: what minimum catalogue of states would be sufficient to justify us in saying that there is no change without a change in positions or states?

Thus take primitive atomic theory. Atoms are posited, small analogues of the primordial bodies. Here, as in the positing of sets or other mathematical objects, one motive is simplification of the overall system of the world. But here we may recognize also the deeper motive of fixing the notion of a physical difference, a physical state. According to primitive atomic theory with its uniform atoms, any physical difference is a difference in the number or arrangement or trajectories of the component atoms.

Physicalism, on these terms, would say that where there are no such atomic differences there are no differences in matters of fact—and in particular no mental differences. But it would never have held out hope of actually describing mental states or even most gross bodily states in terms of the number, arrangement, and trajectories of atoms.

Atoms have since given way to a bewildering variety of elementary particles. Latter-day physicists have been finding even that the very notion of particle is inappropriate at points; paradoxes of identification and individuation arise. There are indications that the utility of the particle model, the extrapolation of the primordial body into the very small, is now marginal at best. A field theory may be more to the point: a theory in which various states are directly ascribed in varying degrees to various regions of space-time. Thus at last bodies themselves go by the board—bodies that were the primordial posits, the paradigmatic objects most clearly and perspicuously beheld. *Sic transit gloria mundi.*

What then is the brave new ontology? There are the real numbers, needed to measure the intensity of the various states, and there are the space-time regions to which the states are ascribed. By identifying each space-time point with a quadruple of real or complex numbers according to an arbitrary system of coordinates, we can explain the space-time regions as sets of quadruples of numbers. The numbers themselves can be constructed within set theory in known ways, and indeed in pure set theory; that is, set theory with no individuals as ground elements, set theory devoid of concrete objects. The brave new ontology is, in short, the purely abstract ontology of pure set theory, pure mathematics.[4] At first we just tolerated these abstract objects as convenient adjuncts to our central corporeal ontology because of the power and simplification that they contributed. In the end, like the camel who got his nose under the tent, they have taken over.

A lesson to be drawn from this debacle is that ontology is not what mainly matters. When bodies first came into my story I warned that they, even they, were theoretical. All theoretical entities are here strictly on sufferance; and all entities are theoretical. What were observational were not terms but observation sentences. Sentences, in their truth or falsity, are what run deep; ontology is by the way.

The point gains in vividness when we reflect on the multiplicity of possible interpretations of any consistent formal system. For, consider again our standard regimented notation, with a lexicon of interpreted predicates and some fixed range of values for the variables of quantification. The sentences of this language that are true remain true under countless reinterpretations of the predicates and revisions of the range of values of the variables. Indeed any range of the same size can be made to serve by a suitable reinterpretation of the predicates. If the range of values is infinite, any infinite range can be made to serve; this is the Skolem-Löwenheim theorem. The true sentences stay true under all such changes.

Perhaps then our primary concern belongs with the truth of sentences and with their truth conditions, rather than with the reference of terms. If we adopt this attitude, questions of reference and ontology become quite incidental. Ontological stipulations can play a role in the truth conditions of theoretical sentences, but a role that could be played as well by any number of alternative ontological stipulations. The indecisiveness of ordinary language toward questions of reference is the more readily excused.

What now of physicalism? To profess materialism, after all this, would seem grotesquely inappropriate; but physicalism, reasonably reformulated, retains its vigor and validity. Our last previous formulation came to this: there is no difference in the world without a difference in the number or arrangement or trajectories of atoms. But if we make the drastic ontological move last contemplated, all physical objects go by the board—atoms, particles, all—leaving only pure sets. The principle of physicalism must thereupon be formulated by reference not to physical objects but to physical vocabulary. Let us take stock of the vocabulary.

Our language still has the standard regimented form: there are the truth functions, the quantifiers and their variables, and a lexicon of predicates. The variables now range over the pure sets. The predicates comprise the two-place mathematical predicate 'ϵ' of set membership and, for the rest, physical predicates. These will serve to ascribe physical states to space-time regions, each region being a set of quadruples of numbers. Presumably regions are always wanted rather than single points—sometimes because of indeterminacy at the quantum level and sometimes for more obvious reasons, as in the case of temperature or entropy. A state may be ascribed outright, for example leftward spin, or quantitatively, for example temperature. In the one case the form of predication is

'*Fx*', combining a one-place predicate and a variable whose relevant values are sets of quadruples of numbers. In the other case the form is '*Fxy*', combining a two-place predicate and two variables. The relevant values of one of the variables are again sets of quadruples of numbers, and those of the other variable are single real numbers measuring the quantitative state. Thus this two-place predicate '*F*' might read 'the temperature in degrees Kelvin of the region . . . is . . . '. Also there may by polyadic predicates ascribing relations, absolute or quantitative, to pairs of regions, or to triples, or higher. In any event the lexicon of physical predicates will be finite, such being the way of lexica.

A nice contrast emerges, incidentally, between physical law and physical description. The laws favor no specific space-time regions as values of the variables. Thus they are independent of the parochial specificity that goes into our choice of spatio-temporal coordinates. The specificity shows itself only in more mundane pursuits such as astronomy, geography, and history, where it is welcome.

But this is by the way. What now is the claim of physicalism? Simply that there is no difference in matters of fact without a difference in the fulfillment of the physical-state predicates by space-time regions. Again this is not reductionism in any strong sense. There is no presumption that anyone be in a position to come up with the appropriate state predicates for the pertinent regions in any particular case.

This formulation, 'fulfillment of physical-state predicates by space-time regions', is decidedly unfinished. The space-time regions are sets of quadruples of numbers, determined according to some system of coordinates that I have not paused over. The physical-state predicates are the predicates of some specific lexicon, which I have only begun to imagine, and which physicists themselves are not ready to enumerate with conviction. Thus I have no choice but to leave my formulation of physicalism incomplete. I suggested before that a major purpose of physics has been to find a minimum catalogue of states—elementary states, let us call them—such that there is no change without a change in respect of them. This is true equally of physics today.

In conclusion I want to relate physicalism to my perennial criticisms of mentalistic semantics. Readers have supposed that my complaint is ontological; it is not. If in general I could make satisfactory sense of declaring two expressions to be synonymous, I would be more than pleased to recognize an abstract object as their common meaning. The method is familiar: I would define the meaning of an expression as the set of its synonyms. Where the trouble lies, rather, is in the two-place predicate of synonymy itself; it is too desperately wanting in clarity and perspicuity.

Translation proceeds, presumably, by interlinguistic equivalence of synonymy of sentences. So, in order to make the problem of synonymy graphic, I developed a thought experiment in radical translation—that is, in the translation of an initially unknown language on the strength of behavioral data.[5] I argued that the translations would be indeterminate, in the case of sentences at any considerable remove from observation sentences. They would be indeterminate in this sense: two translators might develop independent manuals of translation, both of them compatible with all speech behavior and all dispositions to speech behavior, and yet one manual would offer translations that the other translator would reject. My position was that either manual could be useful, but as to which was right and which wrong, there was no fact of the matter.

My present purpose is not to defend this doctrine. My

purpose is simply to make clear that I speak as a physical-ist in saying there is no fact of the matter. I mean that both manuals are compatible with the fulfillment of just the same elementary physical states by space-time regions.

Radical translation proceeds in the light of observed behavior, and behavioral criteria will ordinarily decide in favor of one translation rather than another. When they do, there is emphatically a fact of the matter by micro-physical standards; for clearly any difference in overt behavior, vocal or otherwise, reflects extravagant dif-ferences in the distribution of elementary physical states. On the other hand my doctrine of indeterminacy had to do with hypothetical manuals of translation both of which fitted all behavior. Since translators do not supplement their behavioral criteria with neurological criteria, much less with telepathy, what excuse could there be for sup-posing that the one manual conformed to any distribution of elementary physical states better than the other man-ual? What excuse, in short, for supposing there to be a fact of the matter?

We have here an illustration of what I consider the proper function of behaviorism. Mental states and events do not reduce to behavior, nor are they explained by behavior. They are explained by neurology, when they are explained. But their behavioral adjuncts serve to specify them objectively. When we talk of mental states or events subject to behavioral criteria, we can rest assured that we are not just bandying words; there is a physical fact of the matter, a fact ultimately of elementary physical states.

We learn mentalistic idioms, like other idioms, from elder speakers of our language, in distinctive and inter-subjectively observable circumstances. Those circum-stances differ from others in respect of the distribution, however inscrutable, of elementary physical states. As

long as we use such an idiom in a form and in circumstances closely similar to the original ones, we communicate information; there is a fact of the matter. But our
mentalistic idioms, like other idioms, go on growing and
stretching by analogy. Factual content becomes meanwhile more tenuous and more elusive and can disappear
altogether.

Thus consider the propositional attitudes; consider
belief. There are unproblematical attributions of belief—
unproblematical attributions even to dumb animals.
Observation of behavior would normally prompt us to
agree that the dog believes his master is coming, or that
he believes the ball is under the sofa. When we attribute a
belief about ancient history to someone, on the other hand,
we are dependent on what he says—even though we are
loath to equate belief with lip service. If the believer is a
foreigner, our attribution may be subject also to the
vagaries of translation of his testimony into our language.
In some cases factual content is lacking; in others it is
sparse and ill defined.

I do not advise giving up ordinary language, not even
mentalistic language. But I urge awareness of its pitfalls.
There is an instructive parallel between questions of
reference, on the part of ordinary language, and questions
of factuality. Let me recall what I said earlier when dis-
cussing ontology. Ordinary language is only loosely
referential, and any ontological accounting makes sense
only relative to an appropriate regimentation of language.
The regimentation is not a matter of eliciting some latent
but determinate ontological content of ordinary language.
It is a matter rather of freely creating an ontology-oriented
language that can supplant ordinary language in serving
some particular purposes that one has in mind.

Now factuality is similar. Ordinary language is only
loosely factual, and needs to be variously regimented

when our purpose is scientific understanding. The regimentation is again not a matter of eliciting a latent content. It again is a free creation. We withdraw to a language which, though not limited to the assigning of elementary physical states to regions, is visibly directed to factual distinctions—distinctions that are unquestionably underlain by differences, however inscrutable, in elementary physical states. This demand is apt to be met by stressing the behavioral and the physiological.

Within these limits there is still much scope, of course, for better and worse. The terms that play a leading role in a good conceptual apparatus are terms that promise to play a leading role in causal explanation; and causal explanation is polarized. Causal explanations of psychology are to be sought in physiology, of physiology in biology, of biology in chemistry, and of chemistry in physics—in the elementary physical states.

Footnotes

1. See W. V. Quine, *The Roots of Reference* (LaSalle, Illinois, Open Court, 1973), for a speculative account of the steps involved.

2. See Hilary Putnam, "Mathematics without Foundations," *Journal of Philosophy*, Vol. LXIV (1967), 5–22.

3. See Donald Davidson, "Mental events," Lawrence Foster and J. W. Swanson, eds., *Experience and Theory* (Amherst, University of Massachusetts Press, 1970), 79–101; "The material mind," P. Suppes et al., eds., *Logic, Methodology, and Philosophy of Science*, Vol. IV (Amsterdam, North-Holland Publishing Co., 1973), 709–22.

4. I develop the point a little more fully in "Whither physical objects?", *Boston Studies in the Philosophy of Science*, Vol. XXXIX (1976), 303–10.

5. In *Word and Object* (Cambridge, Technology Press of the Massachusetts Institute of Technology, 1960), Chapter 2.

Contributors

ROLAND A. DELATTRE is associate professor and chairman of the Program in American Studies at the University of Minnesota, Minneapolis.

A. ROBERT CAPONIGRI is professor of philosophy at the University of Notre Dame.

MAX H. FISCH is adjunct professor of philosophy at Indiana/Purdue University at Indianapolis and professor emeritus at the University of Illinois.

PETER FUSS is professor of philosophy at the University of Missouri, St. Louis.

FREDERICK A. OLAFSON is professor and chairman of the Department of Philosophy at the University of California, San Diego.

WILLARD VAN ORMAN QUINE is Edgar Pierce Professor of Philosophy at Harvard University.

Index